920
Mcp

McPherson, Stephanie

E

Wilbur & Orville Wright :
taking flight

DATE DUE			
MAY 0 1			

WILBUR & ORVILLE WRIGHT

WILBUR
& ORVILLE
WRIGHT
TAKING FLIGHT

Stephanie Sammartino McPherson
& Joseph Sammartino Gardner

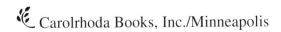 Carolrhoda Books, Inc./Minneapolis

To Dick, whose love, support, and humor keep my spirits soaring
—S.S.M.

To my family, my grandparents, Marion and Angelo Sammartino, my mother, Janis Sammartino, and my brother Jonathan Gardner—for their constant love and support —J.S.G.

Grateful appreciation to Susan Rose for her always insightful editing and to Tim Larson and Tim Parlin for their vision and layout. Thanks to Jennifer McPherson for her usual careful readings of the manuscript and to Marianne McPherson for helping to research and write the section on Orville Wright's conflict with the Smithsonian. A very special thank you to my mother, Marion Sammartino, whose enthusiasm and zest for adventure made our first flight a wonderful experience and to my father, Angelo Sammartino, who explained the principle of aerodynamic lift to me so well in sixth grade that I never forgot it.

—S.S.M.

Carolrhoda Books, Inc., a division of Lerner Publishing Group
241 First Avenue North
Minneapolis, MN 55401 U.S.A.

Website address: www.lernerbooks.com

Library of Congress Cataloging-in-Publication Data

McPherson, Stephanie Sammartino.
    Wilbur & Orville Wright : taking flight / by Stephanie Sammartino McPherson and Joseph Sammartino Gardner.
        p.   cm. — (Trailblazer biography)
    Includes bibliographical references and index.
    Summary: A biography of the brothers who, in 1903, made the first powered, controlled flight in an airplane.
        ISBN: 1–57505–443–4 (lib. bdg. : alk. paper)
      1. Wright, Orville, 1871–1948—Juvenile literature. 2. Wright, Wilbur, 1867–1912—Juvenile literature. 3. Aeronautics—United States—Biography—Juvenile literature. 4. Inventors—United States—Biography—Juvenile literature. [1. Wright, Orville, 1871–1948.
    2. Wright, Wilbur, 1867–1912. 3. Aeronautics—Biography. 4. Inventors.]
    I. Gardner, Joseph Sammartino. II. Title. III. Series.
    TL540.W7M384 2004
    629.13'0092'273—dc21   2002154716

Manufactured in the United States of America
1 2 3 4 5 6 – JR – 09 08 07 06 05 04

Contents

One million people watched, amazed, as Wilbur Wright flew over New York Harbor and along the Hudson River in 1909.

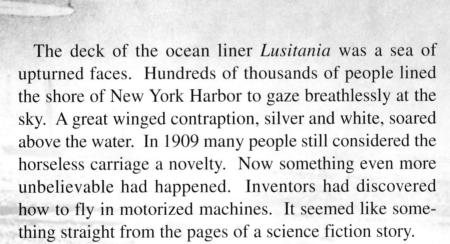

CHAPTER ONE

ALWAYS SOMETHING TO DO

The deck of the ocean liner *Lusitania* was a sea of upturned faces. Hundreds of thousands of people lined the shore of New York Harbor to gaze breathlessly at the sky. A great winged contraption, silver and white, soared above the water. In 1909 many people still considered the horseless carriage a novelty. Now something even more unbelievable had happened. Inventors had discovered how to fly in motorized machines. It seemed like something straight from the pages of a science fiction story.

A red canoe had been strapped beneath the flying machine in case of a sudden water landing. But Wilbur Wright didn't expect any problems as he steered his craft toward the Statue of Liberty. Expertly tilting the wings, he circled the statue at waist level. Ships' bells clanged and whistled. The *Lusitania*'s foghorn blew so loudly that passengers could scarcely hear their own cheers.

In a few moments, the flight was over. Soldiers enthusiastically welcomed Wilbur as he landed on Governor's Island. A quiet man, Wilbur preferred privacy to crowds. But he was passionate about flying and glad to demonstrate the flying machine he had developed with his younger brother, Orville.

As Wilbur climbed from the aircraft, Orville was half a world away, showing off the flying machine to equally excited crowds in Germany. Described by their father as "almost as inseparable as twins," Wilbur and Orville shared every aspect of their work. When they tested their first powered machine at Kitty Hawk, North Carolina, they flipped a coin to see who would make the first flight. Less than ten years later, the Wright brothers had mastered the secrets of flying and become international celebrities.

Not even their parents, Milton and Susan Koerner Wright, could have predicted such success. But they had always believed in all of their children and encouraged them to be creative and persistent. "In a different kind of environment," Orville said, "our curiosity might have been nipped long before it could have borne fruit." Instead, experiments and activities flourished in the Wright household. Although they had little money, Wilbur and Orville always felt they grew up in an educationally privileged household.

Bishop Milton Wright and wife, Susan, delighted in their children's resourcefulness.

Born April 16, 1867, near Millwood, Indiana, Wilbur had two older brothers, Reuchlin and Lorin, who were six and four years older than he was. As the new baby began to grow up, his brothers sometimes tried to boss him around. "I'll squall!" Wilbur threatened when they became too demanding. His words soon became a pet phrase in the family.

The Wright children moved around a great deal while they were growing up. Milton's responsibilities as a preacher in the United Brethren Church took him from Indiana to Dayton, Ohio, where he became the editor of a religious newspaper in 1869. After renting a house for several months, he decided to purchase a home and settle down.

Number 7 Hawthorn Street was crammed onto a narrow patch of land, only two feet away from the house to the north. There was scarcely space for a person to squeeze between the two buildings. But the house was full of laughter, books, and simple comforts. Coal stoves kept the children warm during the harsh winters, and oil lamps gave off enough light to play and read. And the house had room to accommodate the growing family. Although twins Otis and Ida died as babies, Wilbur became a big brother when Orville was born on August 19, 1871. Three years later, Katharine was born on Orville's birthday.

As the children grew up, Wilbur liked to trail along after Reuchlin and Lorin, but he spent lots of time with Orville too. Sometimes he teased his younger brother until Orville chased him furiously, but Wilbur could also

Reuchlin and Lorin Wright as boys. The Wrights chose unusual names for their children because they felt *Wright* was a very common last name.

WILBUR   ORVILLE   KATHARINE

Wilbur at age eight; Orville at age four years, nine
months; and Katharine Wright, three years later, at
age four

be understanding. He made up lively stories to amuse
Orville and let him tag along when the older boys roamed
the neighborhood. In turn, Orville paid lots of attention
to Katharine. He included her in his games and took her
for rides down the street in his wagon.

When he wasn't playing or exploring with the gang,
Orville was often scheming to make a little cash. Milton
said that the children should earn their own spending
money, and there was so much that Orville liked to buy—
especially candy. Occasionally he borrowed from
Wilbur, but one day Orville and a friend hatched a plan
they thought would solve all their money problems. They
scoured the neighborhood, gathering old bones that
people had tossed into their yards or alleys. Then they
hauled their bulky collection to the fertilizer factory.

They were certain the owner would pay a fine sum for so many bones. Instead they received only three cents. There had to be easier ways to make money!

One way was simply wiping the dinner dishes. Susan Wright offered her children a penny a night for this easy task. She also gave them jobs fixing small household items—even though she didn't really need this kind of help. Susan handled tools like an expert. She could mend anything. Better yet, Susan could build toys. The children's favorite was the sled she designed one winter.

Unlike his wife, Milton Wright was all thumbs when it came to simple mechanics. But he was an outstanding churchman. In 1877 he was elected a bishop, a position that required lots of travel, from the Mississippi River to the Rocky Mountains. For a year, the family stayed in Dayton. Finally they moved to Cedar Rapids, Iowa, so Milton could make his trips more easily.

It didn't take the children long to feel at home in their new community. Almost immediately seven-year-old Orville organized a small "army" of fifteen or so boys, appointed himself leader, and made eleven-year-old Wilbur military adviser. The army's imaginary exploits thrilled Orville. Placing his hands on the back of a chair, he kicked his heels in the air as he shared his adventures with his mother.

Milton Wright, tickled by Orville's excitement, enjoyed hearing about the escapades in between his travels. One day Milton came home from a trip with a special present that he casually flung toward Wilbur and Orville. Reaching out to catch the small object, the boys were

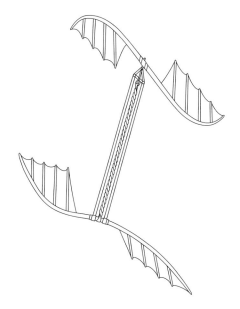

A drawing of a toy helicopter similar to the one Milton Wright gave to Wilbur and Orville. Popular in the mid-1800s, the toy was designed by Alphonse Pénaud.

astounded to see it whirl up to the ceiling. It hovered for several seconds, then spiraled slowly down. Eagerly the boys scrambled to claim the gadget. A toy that could fly! This was better than any plaything they owned.

Their father called the tiny invention a helicopter, but Wilbur and Orville soon dubbed it "the bat." Over and over again, they tightened the rubber bands that sent the bamboo, cork, and paper bat spinning upward. After many flights, the fragile device finally broke.

Not long afterward, Orville slouched over his desk, hoping to hide what he was doing from his first-grade teacher's watchful eyes. But Miss Palmer spotted the wooden sticks in his hand and asked for an explanation. It was a flying machine, Orville admitted. This was only a small one. But if he had made one large enough, he and his brother would be able to fly together!

No doubt his classmates snickered at such silliness. Miss Palmer merely told Orville to put his project away. There would be no demonstrations of flying machines at school. At home, however, there were plenty of opportunities. Wilbur and Orville made several small replicas of the bat, which worked fine. The problem came when they built larger models. Although they copied the proportions of the original bat, the bigger helicopters refused to fly. Disappointed, the brothers turned to other things.

When Wilbur was fourteen and Orville almost ten, their father lost his position as bishop. The family moved to Richmond, Indiana, where Milton became a presiding elder, traveling often to visit church members in the large area assigned to him. Wilbur and Orville's mother had grown up on a farm near Richmond, so they had a chance to see their widowed grandmother often. They also had a chance to explore the buildings scattered around the farmyard

Wilbur and Orville made careful plans to enlarge their toy, the cherished "bat."

where their grandfather's machines and tools were still kept. Much more than a farmer, Grandfather had been a wheelwright who made wagons and carriages. His large lathe, a machine used to shape small logs and blocks of wood, fascinated Wilbur and Orville. Soon they decided to make a lathe of their own in the barn behind their house.

Like their mother, both boys were mechanically talented. Carefully they studied the way the pieces of the lathe were put together and how they functioned to do their job. Then they created their own pieces and fit them together like a giant puzzle. Friends huddled around to watch them work and to try out the foot pedal that powered the seven-foot-long machine.

After making some adjustments, the boys started up the lathe for its final test. A terrible racket filled the room. The barn started to quake and tremble. Could their lathe really be that strong?

Rushing outside to investigate further, Orville gasped in astonishment. The lathe had nothing to do with the disturbance. A small cyclone had touched down in the yard. The wind generated by its fierce spinning pressed Katharine helplessly against the house. To Orville's relief, the storm soon released its grip on his sister.

With their energy and imagination, the brothers never ran out of things to do. Orville built kites to sell to his friends and became an expert kite flier himself. He made chewing gum by sweetening tar with sugar and wrapping it in small bits of paper. But when Orville and a friend actually chewed the gum, they got sick. Abruptly their plans for a thriving business vanished.

Orville soon came up with a better idea to make money. His friend Gansey's father liked to preserve dead birds and wild animals. Why not display these fine-looking specimens at an amateur circus?

Orville's plans for a circus parade and show intrigued fifteen-year-old Wilbur. Half teasing, he offered to write an advertisement. Wilbur may have exaggerated a bit when he called the circus "colossal" and "stupendous," but his vivid phrases captured the fancy of a newspaper editor. After the story appeared in print, so many children turned up for the circus that they couldn't all squeeze into the barn.

Wilbur was quieter than his brother. He loved to read, and he did not need special projects to make cash. Wilbur earned his spending money simply by helping his father with the church newspaper. When folding the papers became too tedious, he invented a device to do the job for him. Although the brothers no longer did everything together, Wilbur took a keen interest in whatever Orville tried. He noted Orville's growing fascination with wood engravings. Orville had first seen pictures printed from carved wood blocks in *Century* magazine. With an old pocketknife, he tried to etch pictures in blocks of wood too. The task became much easier when Wilbur gave him special engraving tools for Christmas. Orville learned to cut images deep into the wood. Applying ink to the wood, he used a small letterpress machine that his father owned to print the pictures.

As Orville pursued his interest in printing and Wilbur prepared to graduate from high school, their father made a decision. He could best serve the United Brethren

Church back in Dayton, Ohio. The family moved in June 1884, before Wilbur, a high school senior, had a chance to go through his graduation ceremony.

The Wrights adjusted well to the familiar surroundings even though their house on Hawthorn Street was occupied by tenants. The family rented another place for the next sixteen months and renewed old friendships. Orville was especially glad to team up with his grade-school buddy Ed Sines, who had a toy printing press. Although Orville was more interested in printing than in his studies, he did fairly well in school. But he liked to talk and was so full of tricks that the teacher insisted he sit in the front row. Maybe that would keep him out of trouble!

Wilbur also enrolled in high school, though he had enough credits to graduate. He enjoyed his studies, joined a social club with his older brothers, and sang with a strong bass voice. He played football and ran faster than almost anyone in the school. His parents were thinking of sending him to Yale University.

Then one winter day, Wilbur was playing shinny, a game like hockey, on a frozen lake. Suddenly another player lurched out of control, his stick waving wildly. In the confusion, Wilbur was struck on the head and collapsed onto the ice. He didn't seem to be seriously injured, and his family expected a speedy recovery. But instead of getting better, Wilbur slowly got worse. His pulse became irregular, and his stomach ached. Within a matter of weeks, Wilbur changed from a confident athlete and ambitious student into a pale copy of his former self.

CHAPTER TWO

REACHING FOR
A CHALLENGE

Although he didn't realize it yet, Wilbur had reached a turning point in his life. Even when his health improved, he felt discouraged and found little to say to his old schoolmates. He didn't return to high school and rarely spoke of his future.

Besides Wilbur's condition, another cloud hung over the Wright household. Susan had not been well since the family had lived in Indiana. She had a disease called tuberculosis, and it was getting worse. Setting aside his own troubles, Wilbur devoted himself to his mother. He took over her chores and cared for all her needs. Reuchlin and Lorin were already on their own, and Orville and

At age twenty-one, Wilbur faced an uncertain future.

Katharine were at school each day. So Wilbur spent many hours alone with his mother. Always close, the two developed an even deeper bond.

Throughout what would have been his college years, Wilbur continued to nurse his mother. He also read a great deal, followed church politics, and continued to watch Orville's doings with interest. Although shy with strangers, Orville was talkative and outgoing with friends and enjoyed practical jokes. He grew a thick mustache and liked to wear the latest styles in clothing. By contrast, Wilbur paid scant attention to what he wore. Slightly taller than his brother, he had a high, domed forehead and quiet, more formal manners. But the brothers shared a deep family loyalty and a fascination with mechanics. Both were practical and enjoyed a good challenge. And both brought remarkable energy and concentration to any project they undertook. Ever since returning to Dayton in eighth grade, Orville had devoted himself to printing. Some of his excitement rubbed off onto Wilbur too.

Orville and his friend Ed Sines set up their own printing business in the Wrights' barn behind their house. Neighbors and acquaintances came to them with all sorts of jobs, from advertisements to tickets to business cards. The boys hired an assistant and bragged that their prices were the cheapest in town.

Orville, who wanted to be a first-rate typesetter, was very careful in arranging small letters on a tray or sheet to be used in printing a page. But he knew he needed more experience. So for two summers, Orville worked in a professional printing shop. When he wanted a bigger and better press of his own, he enlisted Wilbur's help to make one. The brothers began with parts of an old baby buggy, pieces of scrap metal, and a flat bed of rock that had once been a tombstone. They ended with a working press that did exactly what Orville had wanted.

By the spring of 1888, however, sixteen-year-old Orville wanted a faster, better press. Once again Wilbur helped him assemble a collection of odd parts into an efficient machine. They built the framework from pieces of firewood, and they used the folding bars from the top of a buggy to exert even pressure as the type was pressed against the paper. Ignoring conventional rules, Wilbur relied on his own ability to break down a goal into smaller problems and to see to the heart of each one. Word of his originality spread. "Well, it works, but I certainly don't see how it does work," a visiting printer said.

Orville liked to think big. With his fast new press, the seventeen year old established a weekly newspaper. Renting a small office, he found business owners willing to pay for ads in his paper. Orville issued the first copy of the *West Side News* on March 1, 1889. He filled the paper with amusing incidents and jokes as well as neighborhood events. People enjoyed reading it. Soon Wilbur began contributing entertaining pieces too. In fact, Wilbur worked so hard that Orville named him the paper's editor.

Despite his growing involvement with Orville's activities, Wilbur never neglected his mother's needs. When Susan Wright died on July 4, 1889, a grieving Milton described Wilbur's careful nursing in his journal. "Such devotion of a son has never been equaled. . . . Her life was probably lengthened, at least two years, by his skill."

Orville's schoolmate, Paul Lawrence Dunbar, became a famous African American poet. He wrote a poem describing the *West Side News* as, "A sheet that's newsy, pure and bright--/Whose editor is Orville Wright."

Wilbur's anguish spilled over into the obituary he wrote with Orville for their newspaper. "Her children have lost their best, their truest friend on earth," he declared.

That September Orville should have started his last year in high school. Yet even before his mother's death, Orville had decided he would leave school and concentrate on his press and his paper. Publishing a newspaper was demanding, exciting work. Within a year, Orville and Wilbur were ready to look farther afield for news and to publish every day instead of once a week. Canceling the *West Side News,* they announced that the new *Evening Item* would print "all the news of the world that most people care to read, and in such shape that people will have time to read it."

These were ambitious words. Struggling to meet deadlines and to keep their commitment to excellence, the brothers were constantly on the go. They highlighted local problems, pointing out the need for street and sewer repairs and improved streetcar service. A news service kept them up to date on international events. Wilbur also wrote pieces urging readers to support voting rights for women and to oppose American involvement in foreign affairs.

For almost four months, Wilbur and Orville produced their small newspaper. But Dayton had twelve other newspapers with better equipment and more money. Although the brothers worked as hard as they could, they didn't make enough money to stay in business. Reluctantly they returned to printing small jobs, such as business cards or advertisements for individuals.

At twenty-three and nineteen, the Wright brothers had time and energy to spare. It didn't take them long to find

The "safety" bicycle *(right)* was a big improvement over the awkward-riding "ordinary" bicycle *(below)*.

a new interest—cycling. People weren't riding "ordinary" bicycles anymore, with their enormous front and tiny rear wheels. Instead, the new "safety" bicycle was all the rage. It had two wheels of the same size, so it was lower than the ordinary bicycle and much more comfortable to ride. Newspapers were hailing the safety bicycle as "a national necessity" and "a boon to all mankind." In 1890 Orville spent $160, a huge sum of money, to buy a bicycle. With an eye for a bargain, Wilbur found a bicycle for half that amount.

The brothers loved to pedal around the countryside and meet friends. Even better, Orville loved to race. The faster he went, the more competitive he became. He even won several medals.

SPRINGFIELD BICYCLE CLUB.

BICYCLE CAMP-EXHIBITION & TOURNAMENT.
SPRINGFIELD, MASS. U.S.A. SEPT. 18. 19. 20. 1883.

Bicycle racing, a popular event in the late 1800s, became Orville's favorite sport.

Because the Wright brothers had a reputation as mechanical wizards, friends sometimes asked for their help when their bicycles broke down. That gave the brothers a great idea. In 1892 twenty-five-year-old Wilbur and twenty-one-year-old Orville opened a bicycle shop. They worked hard selling and repairing bicycles. But they also had fun. One time they took apart two old-fashioned bicycles that had been traded in for the new safety models. Using the four-foot-high front wheels, they created a gigantic tandem bicycle, a bicycle built for two. People stared open-mouthed as they pedaled their super machine down the street.

After about three years, the Wright brothers began designing and building their own bicycles for sale. They advertised their new models in the last issue of a small publication they printed called *Snap-Shots*. "We guarantee that no wheel on the market will run easier or wear longer than this one," they declared.

The brothers still lived on Hawthorn Street with their father and Katharine. The only one of the Wright children to graduate from college, Katharine was outgoing and interested in all her brothers' activities. She supervised the household and taught Latin and English at Steele High School in Dayton. Wilbur and Orville wanted a comfortable home for their sister and father as well as for themselves. Getting out their tools, they built a spacious front porch that wrapped around the side of the house.

Wilbur (back row, second from right) and Orville Wright (back row, right) about 1892

They added shutters to the front windows and remodeled the bedrooms. In their spare time, they became first-rate photographers. One picture showed off the fine new fireplace they built in the living room.

By this time, their older brothers and many of their friends had married. Orville developed a close friendship with a young woman named Agnes Osborn, a friend of Katharine's. Dressed in his best suit, Orville played chess with Agnes, took her on boat rides, and played pranks on her. As much as he enjoyed her company, however, the relationship didn't become a lasting romance. Both Wilbur and Orville were happy as bachelors. They relished their roles as uncles and knew just how to entertain

A Wright brothers' photograph of their family home at Number 7 Hawthorn Street, Dayton, Ohio

Katharine Wright (right) and a friend enjoy a fire in the fireplace newly built by Katharine's brothers.

Lorin's four youngsters, who lived with their parents in Dayton. Since their brother Reuchlin had moved to Kansas, Wilbur and Orville saw his children less often. But they felt very close to all their nieces and nephews.

If the brothers felt any discontent at all, it came from their longing for broader opportunities. "Intellectual effort is a pleasure to me," Wilbur told his father, "and I think I would be better fitted for reasonable success in some of the professions than in business." Wilbur wanted to grapple with issues and ideas. The bicycle shop provided an income, but it did not satisfy Wilbur's growing impatience for more creative challenges.

In 1896, the year the Wrights began making their bicycles, a horseless carriage appeared on the streets of Dayton.

Wilbur and Orville spent hours discussing the newfangled vehicle with its owner, their friend Cordy Ruse. Certainly the mechanical car had many problems. Sometimes it even lost parts on the road! Still, Orville feared the new means of transportation would eventually take business away from the bicycle. Maybe they should consider building horseless carriages, he told his brother.

But this wasn't the challenge Wilbur sought. Like many others, he laughed at horseless carriages. "To try to build one that would be any account, you'd be tackling the impossible," he declared. "Why, it would be easier to build a flying-machine."

Despite his joking, Wilbur wasn't really convinced that flying was impossible. He had never forgotten the bat from his childhood or his wonder that a toy could fly. With great interest, he followed the career of Otto Lilienthal, a German pioneer in aviation. For ten years, Lilienthal had experimented and collected a large body of data about flying. He tested what he learned by designing his own gliders and taking to the air himself. Since a glider had no engine, it relied on the power of the wind to stay aloft. Lilienthal hung between the wings of his gliders like a giant bird and swayed his body from side to side to change direction.

Between 1891 and 1896, Lilienthal made almost two thousand short flights. The brothers had even written about one of his earliest flights in their newspaper. Through the years, their fascination with Lilienthal's gliders had grown. It was hard to imagine a greater thrill than coasting above the landscape, free as a bird.

In August 1896, Wilbur learned of Lilienthal's death in a gliding accident. About the same time, Orville became desperately ill from typhoid. There was little to be done but keep him comfortable, feed him a liquid diet, and wait for the sickness to run its course. Orville tossed and turned feverishly. The doctor couldn't even predict that he would live. Throughout September, as an anxious Wilbur sat by Orville's bedside, his mind wavered back and forth between his brother's condition and news of Lilienthal's accident. Was the fallen aviator right that someday human beings would fly? Wilbur yearned to discuss the possibility with his brother.

Otto Lilienthal *(inset and gliding)* in 1895. An inspiration to Wilbur and Orville, Lilienthal made almost two thousand flights over a five-year period.

One group of aviation pioneers believed it best to
build and experiment with full-sized gliders. Octave
Chanute designed this one, piloted by Augustus
Herring, in the 1890s.

CHAPTER THREE

AFFLICTED WITH
A BELIEF

On October 8, Orville sat up in bed. He was still very weak, but the worst was over. He was ready to eat soft foods—and to listen to his brother's ideas.

Wilbur's enthusiasm was contagious. Soon Orville began to imagine human flight too. The brothers had much to discuss besides Lilienthal's tragic death.

In the 1890s, there were three main approaches to the possibility of flight. A few experimenters like Sir Hiram Maxim and Clément Ader had built flying machines with engines, but these had barely left the ground before thumping back down. Other flight pioneers hoped to glean information from launching small models. The third group of investigators attempted to fly in full-sized gliders that relied solely on the wind.

Octave Chanute, about 1896. The Wright Brothers looked to the work of Chanute and others to guide their own aviation experiments.

On May 6, 1896, an unpiloted, compact model designed by Samuel Pierpont Langley had flown three thousand feet through the air over the Potomac River at a speed of twenty to twenty-five miles per hour. Langley was sponsored by the Smithsonian Institution, a research and educational organization in Washington, D.C.

On the heels of this success came a successful glider flight staged by engineer Octave Chanute. In his sixties, Chanute felt he was too old to fly the glider he had designed, so his assistant Augustus Herring tested it instead. At first the results were disappointing. By the end of the summer, however, Chanute and Herring had redesigned the glider so that it had a double set of wings, one above the other. With this so-called two-surface machine, Herring flew above the sand dunes on the south shore of Lake Michigan for 359 feet. The glide lasted about fourteen seconds.

The big question was what would happen next. Wilbur and Orville followed the news and read everything they could find in the Dayton library and the encyclopedia about flying. But there was little material to explain the principles of flight, and there were many other tasks to claim their attention.

Three years passed, and still Wilbur couldn't shake the notion that human flight was possible. Sometimes the idea simmered in the back of his mind as he assembled new bicycles. Other times he pondered the possibility consciously as he lay on the ground with Orville and watched the vultures soar overhead. Fascinated, the brothers studied the shapes of the vultures' wings and the way the birds angled those wings to maneuver through the air. In 1899 Wilbur came across a book about birds that roused their interest all over again. "We could not understand that there was anything about a bird that could not be built on a larger scale and used by man," Orville wrote.

It was time, Wilbur decided, to stop wondering and start acting. He believed it was "only a question of knowledge and skill" until people flew. Why shouldn't he ferret out the facts and develop the abilities himself? Writing to the Smithsonian, Wilbur asked for a list of the most helpful reference books on flying machines.

As soon as he received a reply, Wilbur buckled down to some serious studies. Within a few months, he understood flight mechanics as well as anyone else in the field. Wilbur knew that a practical flying machine had to do more than get off the ground. Three basic needs stood out in his mind. First, there had to be wings with enough lifting power to get the machine into the air. Second, there had to be a strong enough source of power to keep the machine moving.

If the machine dropped below a certain speed, it would fall from the sky. Third, there had to be a way to control the balance and direction of the flying machine in the air.

As early as 1810, an Englishman named Sir George Cayley had identified the same needs. In a series of articles, Cayley detailed the way wings worked to lift a flying machine off the ground. The upper surface of the wing had to be curved, Cayley explained. As the wing moved forward, the air split into two streams—one traveling above the wing and one below. The lower airstream went in a straight line. The other stream, following the upper curve of the wing, had a slightly longer distance to travel. In order to keep up with the lower airstream, it moved faster. This meant that the air above the wing was thinner than the air beneath. The denser air below exerted a greater push on the wing than the air above. This upward pressure was what lifted the wing and the flying machine into the air.

Of course, there were many factors to consider. How curved should the wings be? How big did they have to be to lift a certain amount of weight? Did the angle at which they struck the air, the angle of attack, make a big difference? Otto Lilienthal, who had studied air pressure and airflow around different shaped surfaces, had developed guidelines to answer many of these questions.

Wilbur knew that steam and gasoline engines already existed that would provide enough power to propel a flying machine at a steady speed. It seemed to him that the first two requirements for human flight presented no major obstacles. But what about the third? Wilbur found

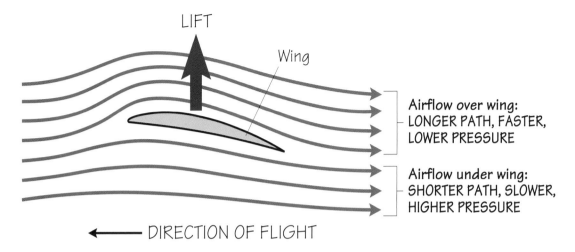

LIFT

Wing

Airflow over wing:
LONGER PATH, FASTER,
LOWER PRESSURE

Airflow under wing:
SHORTER PATH, SLOWER,
HIGHER PRESSURE

← DIRECTION OF FLIGHT

Slower moving, denser air flowing below the wing exerts
an upward pressure that lifts the wing into the air.

very little in his readings about how to control a flying
machine in the air. What good was a machine that would
roll aimlessly through the sky or that could not be maneu-
vered to reach a chosen location? The secret to flight,
Wilbur decided, was to find a reliable means of control.

Wilbur became even more interested in the way birds
circled and darted through the air. When a bird changed
direction, it used its wingtips. If the right wingtip tilted
upward, the left wingtip tilted down. This set the bird
turning in a wide arc. After completing all or part of a
turn, the bird reversed its wingtips and began to turn in
the opposite direction. It was as if the bird became "an
animated windmill," Wilbur explained. The insight
haunted him as he watched birds swooping through the
sky. Wilbur knew he'd discovered the key to flight control. If only he could make the wings of a flying machine
act like the wings of a bird!

Even as he dreamed, Wilbur continued making bicycles. One July day, as he chatted with a customer, he absent-mindedly twisted an empty box that had held an inner tube. The sturdy cardboard did not lose its firmness, but the open ends flexed up and down—in opposite directions.

Suddenly Wilbur realized that he had just done with the ends of the box what he wanted to do with the wings of a flying machine. The solution to his problem lay right in the palms of his hands! Instead of keeping the wingtips separate, he would connect them. The wires joining them would allow the wingtips to tilt in opposite directions— just like the ends of the cardboard box.

Within days the brothers began making a kite to test Wilbur's idea. Built with double wings, like Octave Chanute's glider, the kite was made of pine boards and covered with cloth. The curved wings were connected so

Wilbur at work in the bicycle shop. The Wrights moved to another location when their business expanded.

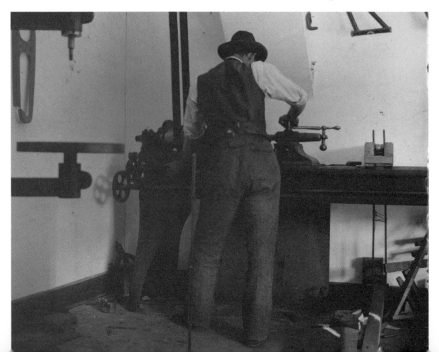

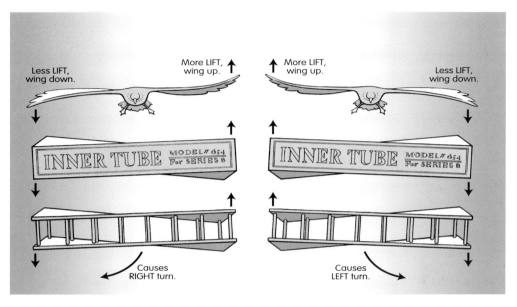

The flaps on a twisted cardboard box gave Wilbur an idea for how to control a flying machine in the air.

that a movement on one side produced an opposite movement on the other side.

Although the brothers were partners, Wilbur did the bulk of the work himself. When he finished the kite, Orville was away on a camping trip. Wilbur couldn't wait to see how well his ideas worked. On the first clear, breezy day, he went out to fly the kite without Orville.

Children gathered to investigate the surprising sight. Dressed in his usual suit and tie, balding thirty-two-year old Wilbur seemed an unlikely person to be playing in a field. Even stranger than Wilbur's serious appearance was the enormous kite itself—and the way it rose and dove and turned and circled. Wilbur directed everything the kite did by moving the sticks attached to the kite's strings. But he had a lot to learn about handling the kite.

Misjudging a dive, he sent the kite plunging toward some small boys. The terrified youngsters threw themselves to the ground as the kite skimmed over their heads. Soon, however, Wilbur had the kite rising in the air again.

For the most part, the kite did exactly what Wilbur hoped it would. Excitedly he hurried to the campsite to share the news with Orville. Now the brothers knew how to control a flying machine from the ground. Could they make a glider that would allow a pilot to direct his course in flight? It was a challenge neither brother could resist.

Wilbur and Orville worked fast. A few months later, by September 1899, they had drawn up rough plans for a glider that would carry a pilot. They figured out how big to make the wings and how much to curve them. They also decided to place a horizontal surface ahead of the wings to help maintain stability and to increase lifting power.

Before Wilbur and Orville could build a flying machine, however, they had to make some more bicycles. By the time they had built enough bicycles for the next cycling season, it was already the spring of 1900. That meant it was time to start selling bicycles all over again. And they still hadn't constructed their glider or decided where to fly it. The brothers knew that testing their glider in Dayton was out of the question. The wind speeds weren't great enough to sustain a glider in flight. Perhaps another flight enthusiast could give them some suggestions.

On May 13, 1900, Wilbur sat down to write to Octave Chanute. "For some years I have been afflicted with the belief that flight is possible to man," he began, adopting a humorous tone. Wilbur shared a few of his ideas on flying and asked if Chanute could recommend an area with winds of about fifteen miles per hour when it wasn't raining.

Within days Wilbur received a warm, encouraging response. Delighted by Wilbur's enthusiasm and knowledge, Chanute suggested several possible sites for testing a glider. Wilbur also wrote to the National Weather Bureau for information about wind speeds throughout the country. But the brothers wanted more than strong breezes. They also needed a place that had hills to take off from and sand for soft landings—a remote place where they could conduct their tests without attracting crowds.

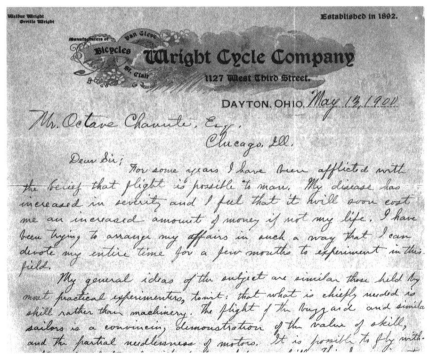

Using his official bicycle shop stationery, Wilbur shared his passion for flying with Octave Chanute.

Studying the list sent by the weather bureau, Wilbur selected a spot that sounded promising and sent for more information from a small beach community on the East Coast.

Two letters arrived in speedy reply, both describing a setting that sounded ideal. The local postmaster assured Wilbur of even more than wind and sand. "This in my opinion would be a fine place," William Tate wrote. "If you decide to try your machine here & come, I will take pleasure in doing all I can for your convenience & success & pleasure, & I assure you you will find a hospitable people when you come among us."

That was all Wilbur and Orville had to hear. They would go to Kitty Hawk, North Carolina.

CHAPTER FOUR

THAT'S HAPPINESS

The Wright brothers had their blueprint and their location. It was time to start building their glider. Again Wilbur took the lead. In the machine room behind the bicycle shop, he steamed pieces of ash wood, then bent them into the right shape to form the curved ribs of the wings. Carefully he crafted other vital pieces out of wood and sewed long panels of shiny sateen cloth to cover the wings. Wilbur planned to take all these parts to North Carolina where he would buy additional supplies, including long spars, supports for the eighteen-foot-long double wings. Then he would assemble the glider on the beach where he planned to test it. Once everything was ready, Orville would join him in Kitty Hawk.

By September 1900, Wilbur had completed what he could do in the bicycle shop. Bishop Wright had often heard his sons excitedly discuss the possibility of human flight. But he was away on church business and knew nothing of the trip to Kitty Hawk or Wilbur's hopes to actually fly. On September 3, Wilbur wrote to give him the startling news. "It is my belief that flight is possible," he explained, "and, while I am taking up the investigation for pleasure rather than profit, I think there is a slight possibility of achieving fame and fortune from it." The bishop's reaction to such startling news can only be imagined.

Just getting to Kitty Hawk was an adventure. On September 6, Wilbur crowded the wooden ribs, his tools, fabric coverings, and even a tent onto the 6:30 P.M. train. The next day, he transferred his unwieldy baggage onto a ferryboat to Norfolk, Virginia. As the temperature inched toward one hundred degrees, Wilbur, in suit and starched collar, trudged through lumberyards in search of eighteen-foot lengths of spruce wood. For all his efforts, the longest pieces Wilbur could find were sixteen-foot planks of pine. Undaunted, he hauled them off to his hotel, then loaded them onto his train the next day. He was bound for Elizabeth City, North Carolina.

Wilbur spent several days combing the wharves of the riverside town looking for someone to take him across the sound to the Outer Banks. He knew that Kitty Hawk was located on this narrow strip of land that paralleled the coastline. But to his chagrin, he couldn't find anyone who knew the way. By luck, Wilbur finally ran into a fisher named Israel Perry who nodded in recognition at the mention of Kitty Hawk. Soon Wilbur was hoisting his lumber and heavy trunk onto a small skiff that would take him to Israel's larger fishing vessel three miles away.

Water seeped through the cracks of the run-down skiff. Both men were forced to bail as they headed down the river. To Wilbur's dismay, the fishing boat was in even worse shape than the skiff. The sails and ropes were rotting away, and the cabin was filthy and "vermin infested," Wilbur wrote home. When a storm arose, Wilbur still couldn't bring himself to enter the grimy cabin. Violent waves buffeted the craft. Several sails broke, and Wilbur's arms and back ached from bailing water. Even Israel was beginning to appear alarmed. Together the men and Israel's young helper managed to maneuver the boat back into the calmer waters of the North River. The next evening after dark, the boat dropped anchor in Kitty Hawk Bay.

The welcome the Tate family gave Wilbur the next morning more than made up for his hardships. For almost two days, he had eaten nothing but jelly from a jar Katharine had packed with his clothes. Gladly he accepted Mrs. Tate's offer of ham and eggs. He arranged to live with the Tates until he could set up a camp on the sand dunes.

Meanwhile, Wilbur borrowed Mrs. Tate's sewing machine so he could shorten the cloth wing covers to fit the shorter wing spars he had bought. He also set up a canvas awning in the front yard where he could start putting together the glider. Intrigued but skeptical, the townspeople didn't know what to make of a grown man working on a flying machine. After all, if God meant people to fly, they thought, wouldn't he have given them wings?

Kitty Hawk camp, 1900. The wind, sand, and isolation of the spot were just what the brothers needed.

Wilbur's own ambitions were simple enough. "I do not expect to rise many feet from the ground," he wrote to his father. When Wilbur had almost finished the glider, Orville arrived on September 28. For several days Orville stayed with Wilbur at the Tates' house and helped with the final assembly details. Then the brothers pitched a tent and set up camp about half a mile away.

In early October, Wilbur and Orville sent their glider up in several unpiloted tests. Watching the machine lift into the wind, Wilbur felt a mounting excitement. He just had to try the glider himself. While Orville and Bill Tate grasped ropes attached to each wing and flew the glider like a kite, Wilbur rode. Lying on the wing fifteen feet above the sand, he felt the wind rush past. Then the glider began to buck up and down like a spirited bronco. "Let me down!" Wilbur shouted. Quickly Orville and Bill pulled in the ropes. "I promised Pop I'd take care of myself," Wilbur explained.

Often the brothers flew the glider with no one aboard. Soon they discovered they had to watch their craft even when it was on the ground. Barely three days into their experiments, a sudden gust of wind hurled the glider into the air and flung it onto the sand twenty feet away. Horrified, the brothers saw that half the machine lay in ruins. It took them three days to rebuild the structure.

Although the 1900 glider could support a person, the brothers often tested it as a kite.

The wind caused other problems too. Several nights a week, the brothers' tent would start to blow away. As they struggled to hold it down, sand blew in their faces, blinding and choking them. A resigned Orville wrote to Katharine, "We came here for wind and sand, and we have got them." Life was certainly rough in Kitty Hawk. Hordes of mosquitoes tormented Wilbur and Orville. Bitter cold nights chilled them to the bone. But the sky glowed with incredible colors at sunset, and the stars were so bright that Wilbur could read his watch by them.

Sometimes Wilbur and Orville added heavy chains to the glider to test its ability to bear weight. Ambitiously they pored over the wealth of data they recorded on each flight. One thing, in particular, baffled them. The glider didn't produce as much lift as they had anticipated, even when they recalculated to compensate for shorter wings. They had expected the glider to fly higher. Wilbur had studied Otto Lilienthal's air pressure tables carefully when he designed the craft. He would have to start all over again, planning a glider with much bigger wings to get the amount of lift he wanted. There were also difficulties with the elevator, the horizontal surface that the brothers had placed ahead of the wings to help control the glider. Wilbur was thoroughly confused. "It is with considerable effort that I have succeeded in keeping him in the flying business at all," wrote Orville, with a bit of exaggeration.

Meanwhile the bicycle business needed their attention. Katharine wrote that she had fired the man hired to tend the shop in their absence. That meant that Wilbur and

Orville would have to return to Dayton soon. They wanted to make the most of the time they had left. Already they had learned all they could from flying the glider like a kite.

Neither brother had yet attempted free flight. On October 20, atop Kill Devil Hill four miles south of their camp, Wilbur lay down in the middle of the lower wing. Orville and Bill Tate each grasped a wing and began racing down the hill into a stiff breeze. As air rushed over the wings, the craft rose a foot or two into the air. Although he barely skimmed the ground, there was nothing to hold Wilbur back. For the first time, he was flying freely into the wind!

Orville and Bill continued to run beside the craft, pushing down whenever a wingtip slanted too far upward. Within several seconds, the glider outstripped the panting men. Wilbur tilted the elevator downward and landed softly.

A dozen or so times, the men lugged the fifty-pound machine back up the hill and repeated the procedure. Again and again, Wilbur climbed back into the glider. His best glides were twenty seconds long and covered three hundred to four hundred feet. By the end of the day, he had spent a total of two minutes in the air. The brothers were delighted. As Wilbur wrote, "We considered it quite a point to be able to return without having our pet theories completely knocked in the head by the hard logic of experience, and our own brains dashed out in the process."

Leaving their flying machine at Kitty Hawk, the brothers returned home and buckled down to building bicycles.

They also wrote to tell Octave Chanute about their recent adventures. The famous engineer was surprised and impressed that Wilbur had flown already. Even more exciting were Wilbur and Orville's plans to return to Kitty Hawk the next year with a much better glider. By May 1901, their blueprints were complete. The new glider would have a wingspan of twenty-two feet, bigger than any glider tested before. Wilbur and Orville could hardly wait to try it out.

Only one thing kept the Wright brothers from leaving at once for Kitty Hawk. They couldn't afford to close their shop during the summer bicycle season. Then, one Saturday evening, an acquaintance named Charlie Taylor stopped by the bicycle shop to chat. How would you like to work for us? one of the brothers asked. Charlie thought he'd like it fine. The pay was good, and he could bicycle home to lunch. "Besides," he said, "I liked the Wrights."

Charlie started work in the middle of June. That gave Wilbur and Orville plenty of time to prepare for their trip and to entertain Octave Chanute, who had come to Dayton to meet them. The acknowledged flight expert brought his new friends a French anemometer—a device for measuring wind speed. It would be useful when they tested their new glider. The three men had a great deal to share. In fact, they talked all through dinner and kept right on talking until Chanute had to leave the next day. Less than two weeks later, the brothers took off for Kitty Hawk.

When the Wright brothers arrived at the site of their previous tests, they saw the fragment of a wing sticking out of the sand. It was all that was left of their 1900 glider.

Wilbur called the new hangar in which the brothers assembled their 1901 glider "a grand institution ... with big doors hinged at the top."

Torrential rains forced them to spend most of their first day huddled under cover. Unable to dig a well, they drank rainwater that trickled down the tent's sides into a dishpan.

Finally the sun came out, and Wilbur and Orville set to work building a hangar for the new glider. Swarms of mosquitoes plagued them. According to Orville, they "almost darken[ed] the sun." Feeling wretched, he wrote to Katharine, "They chewed us clear through our underwear and socks. Lumps began swelling up all over my body like hen's eggs." Wilbur and Orville tried to drive the mosquitoes away with smoke from burning logs. But it was almost impossible to get any relief.

The Wright brothers were not alone in their agony. Octave Chanute had persuaded them to accept two men to be their assistants that summer. Edward Huffaker arrived on July 18 and George Spratt one week later. They were in time to help carry the newly assembled glider up the biggest hill for the first flight of the season. Bill Tate and his half brother Dan were also there for the big occasion.

Always proper, Wilbur wore his usual suit coat, starched collar, and tie as he lay down in the center of the lower wing. Two men grabbed the wingtips and ran down the dune. "Let go!" shouted Wilbur as the glider gained speed. The men did.

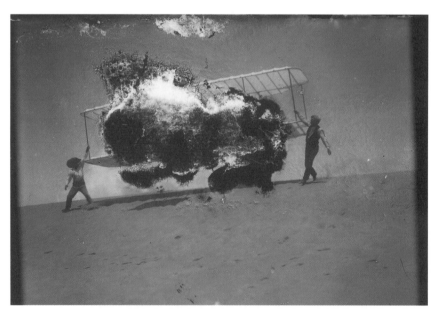

This damaged photo shows Dan Tate *(left)* and Edward Huffaker *(right)* stabilizing the 1901 glider but obscures the pilot, Wilbur. Many of the Wrights' early photographs were damaged during a 1913 flood.

Abruptly the machine dropped, its skids digging into the soft sand. Disappointed but determined, Wilbur tried again—and again. Each time he shifted his weight, hoping to change the center of gravity. Finally on the ninth try, the glider took off. Barely 3 feet off the ground, Wilbur traveled 315 feet in nineteen seconds. The men cheered and hurried down the hill to greet him. But Wilbur felt confused and disappointed. Something was seriously wrong with the glider.

Once more the men trudged up the hill with the glider. On the tenth flight, Wilbur lost control as the glider rose quickly to twenty feet. Then it began to slow down dangerously. Frantically the men yelled directions from below. Wilbur was in the middle of a stall. If he didn't recover quickly, he would plunge to the ground as Otto Lilienthal had done in his fatal accident.

Furiously Wilbur adjusted the front rudder. Instead of crashing, the machine drifted calmly to the ground. Shaken but unharmed, Wilbur crawled from the glider as the men rushed to his side. Already Wilbur's mind was grappling with the near calamity. What had saved him? Things were happening that he didn't understand.

Despite the problems, Wilbur kept right on making glides that afternoon. He stalled a second time. Once again he was able to land safely, but the brothers realized that the glider was much more dangerous than they had thought. As the days went by, they became more disappointed—and scared. Why did the 1901 glider produce even less lift than their previous model? Why was it so hard to control? And what had saved Wilbur when the craft stalled?

Wilbur Wright soars above the ground during one of
the few successful glides with the 1901 glider.

All Wilbur could think about his escape was that the elevator had slowed the glider's fall. But he didn't understand why.

After some tests, Wilbur and Orville made a few changes in the glider's structure. They finished about the time that Octave Chanute arrived in camp for a week's visit. For the first time, the famous engineer saw Wilbur fly. The brothers' improvements had made a difference. In one especially good glide, Wilbur covered almost four hundred feet. But the craft still had problems. One low flight ended in an accident in which Wilbur was pitched forward through the elevator. He suffered a few cuts and a black eye.

Several days later, Wilbur was in the air again, but he couldn't duplicate his best glide. Even worse, lifting power remained poor. Wilbur and Orville were utterly baffled. They had designed the glider according to Lilienthal's tables of air pressure. Could his calculations be wrong? Lilienthal's charts predicted the amount of lift a flying machine should produce based on its wing surface, the angle at which the wing hit the air, and the speed. Without such data, the brothers wouldn't know how big to make their wings or how to shape them to get the amount of lift they needed. Finding the right dimensions would be almost impossible. The mere thought that Lilienthal might be wrong overwhelmed Wilbur and Orville.

When they left camp, Wilbur and Orville were so discouraged they doubted they would ever return to Kitty Hawk. People wouldn't fly in a thousand years, Wilbur muttered. At home on Hawthorn Street, they didn't want to talk about flying at all.

But they did want to develop the film they had taken of their adventures. In their darkroom, pictures slowly formed on the glass plates they had exposed. Breathlessly, Wilbur and Orville watched to see if their glider appeared or if the photographer had missed and all they had was a picture of an empty sky. Whenever they saw their machine soaring, their spirits lifted too. "In the photographic darkroom at home we pass moments of as thrilling interest as any in the field," Wilbur declared.

Despite the exciting photos, the brothers were still confused and unsure of their next step. Octave Chanute had sensed their disappointment and wanted to help them.

He invited Wilbur to speak about flying to the Western Society of Engineers in Chicago. At first Wilbur thought he would decline. He was nervous about speaking before a large audience, and he didn't like to dress up. But Katharine talked him into accepting. She too wanted to see her brothers continue their work.

Doggedly, Wilbur set to work on his speech. He reviewed everything he and Orville had learned. Would the talk be "witty" or "scientific," Katharine wanted to know. "Pathetic," Wilbur replied with gloomy humor. On September 17, he set off for Chicago in Orville's fashionable topcoat, shirt, and cufflinks. A delighted Katharine reported that he looked "swell."

Wilbur gave an honest and informative presentation to the Western Society of Engineers. But he saved one important observation for Chanute alone. He confided his growing belief that Lilienthal's air-pressure tables were wrong. Originally he had wanted to include that statement in his speech, but Orville had talked him out of it. How could the brothers support such a startling claim? Orville demanded. After all, they didn't have the correct figures. Before Wilbur made a public declaration, Orville felt they had better come up with some proof.

When Wilbur arrived home, the brothers devised a simple experiment using a bicycle. They fastened an extra wheel to the handlebars at right angles to the front tire below. The strangely placed wheel could move freely in a breeze. With narrow rods, Wilbur and Orville attached a tiny curved metal wing and a flat wing onto the wheel's rim. They pedaled furiously up and down the streets to increase the force of the wind blowing across the small wings on the bike's handlebars. Sometimes they rode with the breeze, sometimes against it. Carefully they watched to see how the tiny wings, or airfoils, moved in the rush of wind. They also noted the rotations and pauses of the special wheel on which they were mounted. Lilienthal's tables predicted an equilibrium when the wind had tilted the airfoils a certain number of degrees. That meant that the forces should all balance each other and the revolving wheel should remain motionless. But the brothers observed that the wheel wasn't motionless when the tables said it would be. The wings had to tilt at a steeper angle before the balance was achieved. Lilienthal's tables were indeed wrong!

But Wilbur and Orville needed more data than they could get by riding a bicycle. They needed to come up with their own figures. The solution seemed to be a wind tunnel. The brothers built a six-foot-long oblong box with a glass window on top so they could see everything that happened inside. A fan at one end sent a steady stream of air blowing through the tunnel. Strips of wood covered with wire screening were set in front of the fan. This ensured that the air would travel in straight currents. Wilbur and Orville made dozens of tiny metal wings of different shapes and curvature. One by one, they mounted the wings on a delicate balance inside the wind tunnel, turned on the fan, and watched what happened. What shape produced the best lift? What happened when the angle at which the wingtip met the wind was changed? Slowly the brothers acquired answers to these questions.

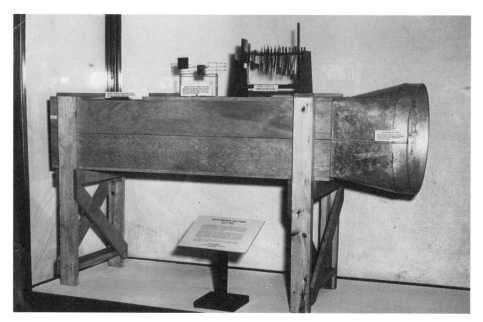

A replica of the wind tunnel the Wrights used to study the flow of air around tiny wings that each had a different shape. The balance arms that held the wings are shown on top of the wind tunnel.

Wilbur and Orville loved every minute of their experiments. They could scarcely wait to try the next shaped wing—and the next. When they went to bed at night, their minds churned with ideas. "Wilbur and I could hardly wait for morning to come to get at something that interested us," Orville said. *"That's* happiness."

But happiness didn't mean that Wilbur and Orville always agreed. As they designed their gliders, they often disagreed fiercely. Seated on either side of the fireplace, they glared and yelled at each other. "'Tis so!"—"'Tisn't either!" Back and forth the charges flew. They argued so well that occasionally they convinced each other in the middle of a discussion. Swapping their original positions, they continued to shout at each other. Wilbur and Orville sharpened their wits and increased their understanding in the lively disputes. "I love to scrap with Orv," Wilbur said. "Orv is such a good scrapper."

By the middle of December 1901, the Wright brothers had all the information they needed. They continued to build bicycles, to design their next flying machine, and to spend time with their nieces and nephews. "Orville never seemed to tire of playing with us," said Ivonette. "If he ran out of games, he would make candy." Wilbur enjoyed playing with the children too, but he often remembered other things to do. If a child sat on his lap too long, he would stretch out his long legs so the youngster could slide down and find another pastime. Their nephew Milton especially loved to play at the shop with its fragrant wood shavings and many interesting gadgets. His uncles never said they were doing anything special.

Wilbur and Orville's nephew and nieces (from left to right) Horace, Leontine, and Ivonette sit on the lap of their father, Lorin Wright, in 1901.

As far as Milton was concerned, flying machines were built in all bicycle shops.

By September 1902, Wilbur and Orville were back at their camp in Kitty Hawk. Determined to live comfortably, they cleaned up their shed, built a kitchen and living room, and made a sleeping area in the loft above. Then they set to work to assemble their glider. All the knowledge they learned from their wind tunnel had gone into the design of the new biplane wings. These wings spanned thirty-two feet and were covered with snug-fitting fabric. The brothers had fixed a vertical rudder in the rear to help with control. To make maneuvering simpler, they devised a wooden hip cradle in which the pilot, or operator, would lie. This would allow the operator to work the wing-warping mechanism by moving his hips.

Would this glider perform better than their disappointing craft of one year earlier? Wilbur and Orville could hardly wait to find out. They began their gliding test from the gradual rise of Little Hill. Signs looked promising. Encouraged, they carried the machine to the top of Big Hill the next day.

A few more flights confirmed their hope. The 1902 glider's lifting power had improved greatly over the 1901 model. The brothers were delighted. It was time for them to start sharing the risks as well as the science. For the first time, Orville tested the glider in the air.

Flying wasn't nearly as easy as it looked. There was a lot to think about when maneuvering a glider. On one flight, Orville forgot to adjust the elevator. Suddenly the machine turned upward, then dropped down to the ground.

When Wilbur reached the tangle of wood, cloth, and wires, he found Orville in the midst "without a scratch or a bruise."

It would take several days to repair the glider, but nothing could dampen the brothers' spirits. "In spite of the sad catastrophe," Orville wrote in his diary, "we are tonight in a hilarious mood as a result of the encouraging performance of the machine both in control and angles of flight."

Shortly after Wilbur and Orville started flying again, visitors began to arrive. First came a curious Lorin Wright, followed by George Spratt, Octave Chanute, and Augustus Herring. The brothers jammed four more bunk beds into their sleeping loft. At night Orville played his mandolin and the men sang along.

While their companions watched and Lorin took pictures, Wilbur and Orville took turns flying. Most glides covered about 150 to 200 feet and lasted eight to twelve seconds. On October 2, they made three glides longer than 500 feet.

This successful glide took place on October 2. When the weather was fine, the brothers could make about twenty-five flights a day.

The tip of a glider wing hits the ground before the rest of the craft, gouging the ground. The Wrights called this problem "well digging."

A jubilant Wilbur wrote to his father, "We now believe that the flying problem is really nearing its solution."

But something still worried and puzzled the Wright brothers. It was an alarming complication that they dubbed "well digging." During a turn, when one wing was higher than the other, the glider would sometimes slide downward toward the lower wing. As the craft plummeted, the tip of the lower wing would hit the ground first, plunging into the sand and creating a small hole, or well. The tail that Wilbur and Orville had added to this year's glider only seemed to make the situation worse. If the Wrights wanted to have a machine they could rely on, they had to figure out exactly what was happening and what they could do about it.

CHAPTER FIVE

THE WHOPPER FLYING MACHINE

The answer came to Orville one sleepless night as he lay in his bunk. The key to maintaining control was the glider's new tail. They had fixed the tail in place so that it couldn't move. What they should have done, Orville realized, was make the tail movable. Then the operator could move the tail to reestablish balance and prevent the sideways sliding that led to well digging.

At breakfast the next morning, Orville shared the inspiration with his brother. Wilbur saw instantly that Orville had hit upon a workable solution. Already Wilbur was imagining the best way to accomplish his brother's plan. The wires attached to the new movable tail should be connected to the wing-warping wires, he suggested. That would make it easier for the operator to control the entire flying machine.

Once the brothers had made their changes to the glider, they had no more problems with well digging. In fact, they could totally manage their craft. That meant they could control three types of movement: (1) roll—the dipping and rising of the wings, (2) pitch—the dipping and

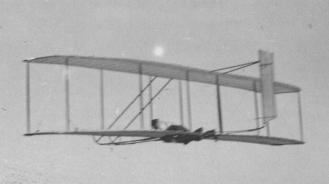

The redesigned 1902 glider had a single, moveable rudder that allowed the operator to control the craft more easily than previous gliders.

rising of the nose or tail, and (3) yaw—the right and left turning movement of the glider in a horizontal surface. Whenever the glider tilted or was buffeted by the wind, Wilbur and Orville had the means to restore balance.

It wasn't until their visitors left camp, however, that the brothers had time to fly as much as they wished. Within a week they made more than 375 glides, many spanning distances of 300 to 500 hundred feet. The best flight of all covered 622.5 feet in twenty-six seconds. "We now hold all the records!" a thrilled Orville wrote home.

When the brothers left Kitty Hawk on October 28, their next step was clear. It was time to install a motor in their flying machine. With a built-in power source, they would not have to depend on the wind to sustain them in flight. Instead of a glider, they would have a true Flyer.

But finding a motor to suit their flying machine proved much harder than Wilbur and Orville expected. They needed a lightweight engine—not more than two hundred pounds. None of the engine companies the brothers contacted wanted the job. They said it was too difficult. Finally, they gave the assignment to their shop mechanic, Charlie Taylor. Together the three men planned the gas-powered motor. As work progressed, one or the other of them would scribble out the rough outline of a part. Charlie pinned the sketches above his workbench. After some trial and error, he produced just the engine the brothers needed.

The brothers needed a way to make the power supplied by the engine push the Flyer forward. For this, they used two propellers that rotated in opposite directions.

A set of chains would connect the propellers to the motor. As the propellers revolved, they would push the air backward. Of course, Wilbur and Orville knew Isaac Newton's Third Law of Motion: For every action, there is an equal and opposite reaction. This meant that as the air was pushed backward, there was an equal and opposite force on the propellers pushing them—and the flying machine—forward. The faster the rotation of the propellers, the stronger these opposing forces would be. The problem was that friction from the air, called drag, resisted the forward motion of the plane. The propellers needed to spin rapidly enough to overcome drag and to create enough thrust to set the plane rapidly moving along the ground. As the plane sped forward, air flowing around the wings created the needed lift to overcome gravity and to carry the plane upward.

Designing the propellers was a tricky job. The brothers had to decide what shape the propeller blades should be, how fast they should turn, and at what degree the whirring blades should hit the air. In their frustration, they still disagreed occasionally and yelled at each other. "Both boys had tempers," Charlie Taylor noted. But they learned from their arguments—they even enjoyed them. Finally they put their knowledge together and devised eight-foot propeller blades. They would be made of three layers of spruce wood glued together. The brothers were excited by their growing knowledge. "Isn't it astonishing," Orville wrote to George Spratt, "that all these secrets have been preserved for so many years just so that we could discover them!"

As usual Wilbur and Orville began building their flying machine in the back room of the bicycle shop. Soon long beams of lumber blocked the hallway leading to the sales area. Whenever someone entered the shop, one of the brothers had to troop outdoors and reenter the shop from the front. The final assembly, of course, would take place at Kitty Hawk. On September 23, the brothers loaded about 650 pounds of equipment onto the early morning train from Dayton and set off.

Arriving at Kitty Hawk, the brothers discovered that a storm had ravaged their camp. They had major repairs to make, and they needed to build a larger shed to house their new craft. But Wilbur and Orville couldn't wait to fly. Even before they assembled their new craft, they began practicing in their previous year's glider. Soon, however, the weather turned against them. A terrible storm pounded the coastline for two days. The roof of their cabin started to blow away. The brothers could scarcely hammer it down as gusts of wind buffeted them.

When the rain finally subsided, Wilbur and Orville seized the chance to glide again. On the second glide, without warning, the wind rose drastically. Orville fell from the sky so quickly that one wing skimmed Wilbur's hair. Two supports broke as the glider hit the ground. Then the storm returned full force while the brothers struggled to get the machine under cover. Belatedly they realized that they had been flying in the eye of a hurricane.

For two more days, they huddled in their quarters. Finally the weather really cleared. They set to work assembling their Flyer. Storms continued to interrupt their progress.

The whopper flying machine wasn't exactly symmetrical.
To balance the weight of the engine *(left center)*, the
right wing was slightly larger than the left.

The cold was bone chilling. Some nights they slept with
five blankets and two quilts. Desperate for warmth during
the day too, Wilbur and Orville hung carpets on the walls
and turned a large metal can into a wood-burning stove. A
dense cloud of smoke filled the room the first time they
used it. The ceiling was coated with ashes. "For several
days we couldn't sit to eat without a whole lot of black soot
dropping on our plates," Orville complained. Eventually,
however, the stove worked well.

Despite the temperature and the sooty food, the brothers continued to work on the new machine and practice gliding in their old model. "We have been in the air hundreds and hundreds of times," Orville told Katharine. But they had still not flown in the motor-driven craft—what they sometimes called "the whopper flying machine." From end to end, the wings measured 40.4 feet across and were covered with a fabric called Pride of the West muslin. They were longer, thinner, and smoother than the wings of the brothers' previous machines. "It is the prettiest [wing] we have ever made," a proud Orville wrote home, "and of much better shape."

It would take more than pretty wings, however, to get the Flyer off the ground. The first time the brothers turned on the motor, the aircraft rattled so much that the propeller shafts developed cracks. These long rods connected the propellers to the Flyer just behind the wings. If they were damaged at all, the propellers might malfunction or even fall off with catastrophic results.

There was no way to repair the shafts at camp, so the brothers sent them back to the bicycle shop for Charlie Taylor to repair. As they waited impatiently, their mood wavered between confidence and deep anxiety. The Flyer weighed about seventy pounds more than they had planned. Would the propellers spin rapidly enough to develop sufficient thrust to lift it from the ground? A brief visit from Octave Chanute didn't help matters much. Chanute thought that the Flyer needed more power than the engine could give. That meant that the propellers would not be able to produce the needed thrust.

Orville humorously compared the ups and downs of his feelings to the rises and dips of the stock market. "Stock in flying machine began dropping rapidly," he wrote one night. "After supper it took a turn for the better."

When the repaired propeller shafts arrived, the brothers revved up the engine once more. The vibrations still shook the Flyer violently. Parts came loose. Finally the brothers had to use bicycle cement to hold some of the components in place. The good news was that the propellers spun much faster than the brothers had dared hope. At speeds of up to 359 revolutions per minute, they produced more than enough thrust to lift the heavier machine. "Stock went up like a sky rocket," a relieved Orville wrote to Charlie Taylor.

Still the Wrights' troubles weren't over. After several more tests, they noticed another slight crack in one of the propeller shafts. Although it was barely visible, the crack could easily widen during flight, causing a midair disaster. There wasn't a moment to lose if the Wright brothers really hoped to make a flight before the end of the year. Soon the winter weather would make flying conditions nearly impossible. On November 30, Orville left for home. He would make the new propeller shafts himself, and he would use spring steel.

Nine days later, Orville was back at Kitty Hawk with two new propeller shafts and some interesting news. On December 8, a flying machine designed by Samuel Pierpont Langley had been tested over the Potomac River. Like the Wright brothers' Flyer, this craft had a motor. Piloted by Charles Manly, the Aerodrome had been launched from the top of a houseboat. Immediately the Aerodrome had plunged into the water. Manly had nearly drowned.

Wilbur and Orville must have thought about the accident as they installed the steel propeller shafts. Although their machine was ready by December 13, the winds were too light to achieve takeoff—even with a motor. Besides, it was Sunday. Although the brothers didn't share all their father's religious views, they respected his beliefs and had promised him that they wouldn't fly on a Sunday.

The first attempt to fly the 1903 machine ended after only 3.5 seconds.

The next day, they couldn't wait to get started. First they lay their new sixty-foot launching track across the sand. A wheeled truck, or dolly, would support the Flyer as it ferried down the track prior to takeoff. The brothers jokingly called it "the Grand Junction Railroad."

Once the track was in place, Wilbur and Orville raised a signal flag to alert the men at a nearby lifesaving station of their intention. If they actually flew a powered machine, they needed witnesses to the event. After several men and two small boys joined them, the brothers flipped a coin to see who would fly first. Wilbur won.

Carefully Wilbur climbed into the Flyer and started down the track. When he came to the end, the machine climbed swiftly to fifteen feet but couldn't continue at its alarmingly steep angle. As rapidly as it rose, it fell from the sky again. Wilbur was not hurt, but the forward elevator and a landing skid were damaged. Neither brother considered the three-and-a-half-second flight a success, but they had learned some important things. The motor worked. The craft had enough power to rise. The launching system did its job. Could they control all these things to make a sustained flight?

On December 17, the brothers were ready to take to the air in their repaired Flyer. The wind blew fiercely. After waiting for it to lessen a bit, Wilbur and Orville just couldn't wait any longer. As before, they raised the flag to summon the lifesaving crew. Since Wilbur had already tried the Flyer, Orville would take the first turn today.

The track was laid, the camera was ready, and the engine was warming. There was nothing left but for Orville to climb into the craft and fly. Although they believed in their machine, anything could happen—as Wilbur's mishap had clearly shown. A member of the lifesaving crew watched the brothers in last-minute conversation. "We couldn't help notice how they held onto each other's hand, sort o' like two folks parting who weren't sure they'd ever see one another again."

The whopper aloft! Wilbur watches as Orville makes the
world's first powered flight at 10:35 in the morning
on December 17, 1903.

CHAPTER SIX

TAKING FLIGHT

Seconds later Wilbur was rallying the men, urging them to look happy and confident for Orville's sake. "We tried to shout and hollo," a witness recalled, "but it was mighty weak shouting with no heart in it." As the Flyer moved down the track, the men roused themselves to run beside it and steady the wings. Sunlight gleaming on its copper wires, the machine rose into the air.

For twelve incredible seconds, Orville jostled and bumped through the air, finally landing on a ridge of sand 120 feet away. Now the men's cheers were for real as they rushed to greet Orville. Short as the flight had been, it was, in Orville's words, "the first [time] in the history of the world, in which a machine carrying a man had raised itself by its own power into the air in full flight."

By the time the men hauled the craft back to the track for another try, they felt numb with cold. Briefly they retired to the brothers' living quarters to warm up before Wilbur made the second successful flight in a powered machine. Orville took the third turn, besting his previous time by three seconds. At noon Wilbur broke the record by flying 852 feet in fifty-nine seconds.

The brothers wanted to try again. They were wondering if they could fly down the coastline all the way to the Kitty Hawk weather station. Without warning, a stiff breeze overturned the Flyer. Frantically the men grasped the craft to hold it down. But the wind was too strong. All but one were forced to let go. John Daniels, a large man, was too tangled in the struts and wires to give up his hold. As the Flyer tumbled across the beach, a terrified Daniels tumbled with it. Wilbur, Orville, and the lifesaving crew pounded after him. When the runaway craft stopped for just a second, Daniels pushed his way out, splintering wood and snapping wires in the process. Although the machine was damaged beyond repair, it had done its job. The brothers would leave Kitty Hawk knowing, as Wilbur said, "that the age of the flying machine had come at last."

Wilbur and Orville rarely let their emotions show. The two brothers walked down the beach to the telegraph station as calmly as if December 17 were the same as any other day. Nothing that happened had really surprised them. "We were simply glad, that's all," Orville explained. "Success," read the first word of their brief telegram home.

RECEIVED at   170

176 C KA C8 33 Paid.   Via Norfolk Va

Kitty Hawk N C Dec 17

Bishop M Wright

            7 Hawthorne St

Success four flights thursday morning all against twenty one mile

wind started from Level with engine power alone average speed

through air thirty one miles longest (57) seconds inform Press

home phays Christmas .   Orevelle Wright   525P

The *Virginian-Pilot* was one of several newspapers to offer an exaggerated account of the Wright brothers' achievement.

Christmas was especially merry that year as the Wrights sat down to a big family dinner at Lorin's house. As usual Wilbur carved the turkey—making a big show of it. He lined up everything he needed at the table and rubbed his hands theatrically to build suspense. Both brothers enjoyed playing with the Christmas toys their nieces and nephews received. The children never minded when they accidentally broke anything. A toy mended by Uncle Will and Uncle Orv worked better than when it was new.

Even as they celebrated, the Wright brothers were thinking ahead to what they would do next. They knew they had reached a crossroads. They could continue to work on flying machines whenever they had the time and money to do so.

Or they could entrust their bicycle business to someone else and concentrate all their time, energy, and money to improving the safety and reliability of their aircraft.

It wasn't a difficult decision. By New Year's Day 1904, the brothers were already working on a new Flyer. Six months later, they were ready to test the new machine in Huffman Field, a pasture they rented about eight miles outside of Dayton. They mowed the grass, chased the cows into a nearby field, and invited reporters to watch them fly on May 23.

Bad weather and bad luck conspired against the brothers. The Flyer never left the ground. A few reporters did watch a very short flight, three days later. But a mere twenty-five feet was not something they could get excited about.

The Wrights with the 1904 flyer at Huffman Prairie. The field was small, forcing the brothers to develop their skills at turning in midair.

Even with a motor, the 1904 Flyer did not maintain momentum in flight well.

After this poor showing, the press basically ignored the Wright brothers.

This situation suited Wilbur and Orville just fine. For several months, they only managed to make very short flights. In fact, they didn't even break their Kitty Hawk record until August 13. They spent a great deal of time just sitting around waiting for a wind strong enough to help lift the flying machine. Despite the motor, whenever the wind slackened, the craft dropped back to the ground. One woman who lived near the field routinely sent her children out with a bottle of lotion for the brothers when she saw the Flyer make a rapid descent. Orville must have welcomed the lotion to soothe his bruises the day he crashed on takeoff. Fortunately he wasn't badly injured. But since the brothers couldn't count on strong, steady breezes the way they had at Kitty Hawk, they realized they would have to invent a new way to launch their craft into the air.

The brothers needed something to make the Flyer move faster on the ground prior to takeoff. This would give them the momentum to stay in the air. Just two weeks after Orville's mishap, they were ready to try their new "catapult launching system." First they hoisted a 1,600-pound weight to the top of a wooden derrick, or tower, twenty feet tall. They attached the Flyer to the weight with a series of ropes and pulleys. To take off, the pilot had to loosen the line that anchored the craft to the ground. Then the weight would descend from the tower, and the Flyer would rush forward along a sixty-foot track. Even with little wind, the machine should begin to rise at the end of the track.

To Wilbur and Orville's satisfaction, the system worked. After they began using the launch tower, they had little trouble getting and staying airborne. Barely one week later, Wilbur flew for a minute and a half, circling Huffman Field completely. Amos Root, a beekeeper who observed the event, called it "the grandest sight of my life." He likened the spectacle to a "great locomotive" with "white wings" leaving its tracks and heading straight toward him!

Despite the dramatic improvement of the launching system, Wilbur and Orville still had a long way to go.

In the best flight of 1904, Wilbur made almost four circles of Huffman Field in five minutes and four seconds. He covered a distance of 2.75 miles.

They still had trouble making turns, and they still had accidents. Hoping to improve safety and control, the brothers made a number of changes in the third powered Flyer they built. The new design gave the pilot more freedom to maneuver in the air. But when they began testing the *Flyer III* in June 1905, they were sorely disappointed. Nothing had changed at all! Almost every day, a new accident damaged their machine. On July 14, Orville lost control and plunged wildly down.

After hitting the ground at thirty miles per hour, the machine continued to bump violently over the ground. Wilbur raced to the scene to find a shaken and bruised Orville entangled in the wreckage of the elevator. But he wasn't badly hurt.

The brothers knew their luck could not last forever. Unless they made some improvements in safety, one of them was going to be seriously injured someday. It took the Wrights a little over a month to figure out what needed to be done and to make the needed adjustments. The remodeled version had a larger elevator at an increased distance from the front of the machine. Would these changes help them direct the Flyer's course? It was time to take to the air again and find out.

CHAPTER SEVEN

ASTOUNDING THE WORLD

Wilbur and Orville flew their remodeled machine again and again. Not a single accident occurred. As they gained skill and experience, they flew for longer and longer periods. On October 5, 1905, Wilbur made thirty circuits around the prairie. A farmer named Amos Stauffer watched in amazement from a nearby cornfield. "The durned thing just kept going round," he declared. "I thought it would never stop."

At last the brothers had a Flyer they could truly count on! Now they faced another crossroads. They could continue to practice flying while they sought buyers. But since they hadn't received patents on their work yet, observers could study their machine and perhaps steal

Orville banks to the left in the last photographed
flight of 1905. Wilbur was age thirty-eight
and Orville was age thirty-four at the time.

their secrets. Rather than risk that, Wilbur and Orville decided to stop flying until they found a business or organization willing to buy one of their machines. They hoped that the United States government would be interested.

Selling an aircraft proved harder than they had expected. Government officials wanted to know how the flying machine worked before they committed themselves to a purchase. But the brothers were afraid to tell them for fear their designs would leak out to competitors.

Besides government skepticism, Wilbur and Orville encountered a great deal of suspicion from the general public. How could they prove their claims when they would not fly or explain how their craft worked? "They are fliers or liars," the Paris edition of the *New York Herald* declared. "It is difficult to fly. It is easy to say 'We have flown.'"

Stubbornly the Wrights stuck to their own terms as they tried to sell their machine. After struggling to present their ideas in the proper form, the brothers finally received a patent in 1906 with the help of an attorney.

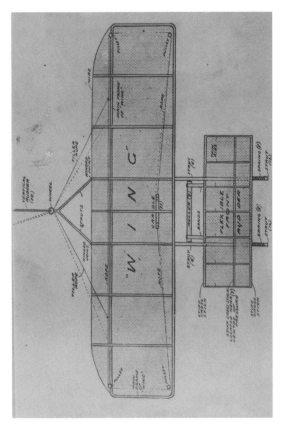

The Wright brothers submitted this diagram of their Flyer, along with others, when they applied for a U.S. patent.

The next year, they visited Europe to scout possible buyers. Soon their claims also received attention in the United States. U.S. Army officials decided to take a more serious look at flying machines and to publish their requirements for considering the purchase of such crafts. The Wrights would have to prove their machine met these government demands. They would also have to convince Europeans that their Flyer did what they said it would. If it took demonstration flights to accomplish this, that's what the brothers would do. With patent protection, they felt more secure in letting others view their work.

Because the army required that a passenger be taken aloft, Wilbur and Orville had abandoned the hip cradle in which they had formerly flown. Instead they installed two upright seats, and the pilot steered with control sticks. The passenger could also reach the sticks, a crucial arrangement when the brothers began teaching others to fly.

But the brothers themselves hadn't flown in almost three years. In April 1908, they returned to Kitty Hawk for some much-needed practice. Wilbur was the first to arrive. The old cabin was almost gone. The roof had caved in, a wall had blown down, and the floor lay under a foot of sand. With the help of several hired men, Wilbur raised a new building in record time. As he was finishing the kitchen, two cars filled with parts of the Flyer arrived. Orville wasn't far behind with a stove, groceries, and the rest of the flying machine.

It took Wilbur and Orville a week to assemble the craft. Then they began flying. One day, after Orville made a thirty-one-second flight, a reporter burst into their camp.

He had meant to stay hidden in the bushes, but the sight of a man flying overwhelmed him so much that he couldn't help himself. In the coming days, the brothers figured out that other reporters were hiding out in the woods to spy on their doings. One writer referred to his colleagues' astonishment: "Men trained to observe details under all sorts of distractions, forgot their cameras, forgot their watches, forgot everything but this aerial monster chattering over our heads."

On May 14, the brothers took up a passenger for the first time. Charlie Furnas, a Dayton mechanic who had come to help out at Kitty Hawk, flew first with Wilbur and then with Orville. The Wright brothers were still learning how to use their new controls. Later that day, Wilbur grabbed the wrong lever and sent the machine plummeting to the ground. Although he wasn't seriously hurt, the aircraft was. To make matters worse, the reporters—who had not actually seen what happened— blew the story out of proportion. Newspapers falsely reported that the Wrights had wrecked their only plane and that they would never be able to meet their commitments to the U.S. government or to a company in France.

Despite these dire predictions, Wilbur and Orville were ready and eager to demonstrate in public what their machines could do. The brothers decided that Orville would stay home to build an aircraft for the army. Then he would make the required test flights at Fort Myer, Virginia. Just three days after his accident, Wilbur left for New York where he would take a ship to France.

On October 7, 1908, at Camp d'Arvours, France, Mrs. Hart Berg became the first woman to fly. The ankle cord *(bottom left corner)* she used to keep her skirt from blowing was widely copied, leading to a new fashion called the hobble skirt.

Several Frenchmen had experimented with their own flying machines and had already flown in public. The French were inclined to doubt the claims of this unknown American who thought he could top their own experiments. In fact, many people thought Wilbur was just plain bluffing. But on August 8, a fair number of people gathered to watch Wilbur take off from a racetrack near the town of Le Mans. Rising to about thirty feet, he traced great arcs in the sky for a minute and forty-five seconds.

Wilbur captivated crowds in Le Mans, France, with his precision flight demonstrations in 1908.

The crowd was stunned. Wilbur flew with a precision that his French rivals didn't come close to matching. "He's not a bluffer." "This man has conquered the air." The words rippled among the spectators as they rushed forward with congratulations. Wilbur had become an instant celebrity.

The following week, Wilbur flew eight times in front of ever growing crowds. The ease with which he completed figure eights over the field left the people flabbergasted. All over France people began talking about the first *hommes-oiseaux*, or birdmen, as the newspapers dubbed

Wilbur and Orville. Even the French army took note and offered Wilbur a nearby rifle range from which to make his flights. Gratefully Wilbur accepted, continuing to make flights that broke records and thrilled onlookers. "They look upon me almost as an adopted citizen," Wilbur wrote to Orville. To his amusement, copies of the old green cap he wore became popular as "Wilbur Wright caps."

But it wasn't just Wilbur's accomplishments that captivated the country. The French were intrigued by the man himself—his openness, broad range of interests, and quiet friendliness. Despite his sudden fame, Wilbur lived simply, sleeping beside his craft in its hangar and doing most of the mechanical work himself. Even when Wilbur was an honored guest at the Aéro Club in Paris, he declined to make a speech. "I know of only one bird, the parrot, that talks," he explained, "and it can't fly very high."

While Wilbur and the Flyer continued to take France by storm, Orville arrived at Fort Myer to satisfy requirements set by the U.S. government for purchasing a flying machine. Several hundred people, including many government officials as well as the president's son, Teddy Roosevelt Jr., watched Orville climb into the aircraft, the afternoon of September 3, 1908. Reports of Wilbur's flights in France had not received much news coverage in America. The people in the crowd hardly knew what to make of the Wright brothers' big claims. As the Flyer reached the end of the track and rose into the air, they gasped in disbelief. Roosevelt Jr. never forgot that "sound of complete surprise" that echoed through the air. Then the spectators burst into applause.

Awed spectators and military officials gaze at the 1908 Wright Flyer soon after Orville's first demonstration flight in September.

When Orville landed after a minute and eleven seconds, the reporters who ran toward him had tears in their eyes. Over the next few days, his flights grew longer, and more and more people flocked to see him. The spectacle of a man soaring above their heads upset all their ideas of common sense and reality. One dazed, well-dressed gentleman wandered through the crowd exclaiming, "My god, my god, my god."

Orville set records, then broke his own records. Just one week after his first demonstration, his flight time had stretched to almost sixty-six minutes. He set an altitude record by flying 310 feet high, and he established another record for the longest passenger flight. Americans went wild. In France, Wilbur wasn't flying nearly as long as his brother. News reporters jumped to the false conclusion that the brothers were staunch competitors. "Whereas a week ago, I was a marvel of skill," Wilbur humorously wrote to Orville, "now [the newspapers] do not hesitate to tell me I am nothing but a 'dud' and that you are the only genuine skyscraper."

On September 11, 1908, Orville Wright further amazed observers at Fort Myer, Virginia, soaring above them for one hour and ten minutes.

One newspaper's account of Orville and Lieutenant
Selfridge's tragic accident in 1908

On September 17, Orville took up his third passenger,
Lieutenant Thomas Selfridge. The flight went fine until
suddenly the men heard two loud thumps. The plane
began to tremble. Orville lost control, and the craft
plummeted to the ground. Both men were rushed to the
hospital by horse-drawn ambulance. Hours later Lieutenant Selfridge died in surgery. Doctors feared that
Orville would die too.

Wilbur was preparing for a flight in France when a cable arrived telling him of the accident. Immediately he canceled the demonstration and retreated alone into the airplane shed. He had no idea how badly his brother was hurt, and he grieved deeply for the young lieutenant. Finally Wilbur bicycled to a nearby town to be closer to the telegraph office. Later that day, a cable informed him that Orville would live. Although he was relieved, Wilbur couldn't shake a terrible feeling of responsibility. "If I had been there, it would not have happened," he told himself over and over again.

A faulty propeller blade was determined to be the cause of the crash. One of the blades had been previously repaired and did not perfectly match the shape of the original blades. That slight difference caused the propeller to revolve off center, snapping one of the lines that positioned the rudder. Despite the accident, army officers were impressed by Orville's previous flights. Although Orville hadn't satisfied all the government requirements, officials believed he had built a sound machine. Before Orville returned home with his sister to recuperate, he promised, "I'll be back next year with a new machine. We will make good on our contract."

CHAPTER EIGHT

DAWN OF
A NEW ERA

In France a lonely but determined Wilbur continued to fly, capturing the imagination of the entire country. He was taking up passengers too. Most of them were well-known people, but Wilbur noticed an ordinary young boy who liked to hang around the flying field. Perhaps the youngster's fascination and longing reminded Wilbur of himself. He took the boy up for a ride. When someone asked why, Wilbur replied, "I took up so and so because so and so wanted me to. I took up this boy because *I* wanted to."

By early 1909, Orville had recovered enough to travel with Katharine's help. The pair joined Wilbur in Paris in mid-January. They met some of the kings, political leaders, and other celebrities who came to watch Wilbur fly.

King Edward VII of England (left) walks with Wilbur (center) and Orville (right) in Pau, France. The king eagerly watched two flights. In one of them, Katharine Wright was taken aloft.

The Wrights found it exciting to be the center of such attention, but it didn't go to their heads. "Kings are just like other nice, well-bred people," declared Katharine.

When they returned to the United States in May, Wilbur, Orville, and Katharine continued to be swamped with attention. Before they docked, they were cheered by passengers on other ships and hailed with whistles and bells. The Wrights had hoped for a quieter arrival in Dayton, but ten thousand people gathered to welcome them back home.

Even that wasn't enough to satisfy those who wished to honor Wilbur and Orville. In mid-June, an enormous celebration was held with fireworks, bands, and a "living flag" of schoolchildren dressed in red, white, and blue. The day after the gala event, the brothers caught the train to Washington, D.C. It was time to complete the two remaining tests for the U.S. Army.

In the first test, Orville had to take a passenger aloft for at least one hour. But when the hour was up, he and Lieutenant Frank Lahm kept right on circling the field. Ten more minutes passed. Orville was about to break the world's record set by his brother in France.

Orville Wright, with passenger Lieutenant Frank Lahm, thrills crowds at Fort Myer, Virginia, on July 27, 1909. President William H. Taft was among the spectators.

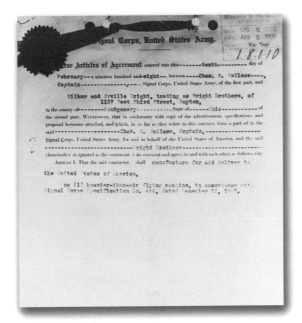

In 1909 the Wright brothers finally landed a contract with the U.S. Army.

The spectators cheered wildly. Usually dignified, Wilbur became so excited that he broke into a dance right in the middle of the field.

To determine how fast the aircraft could go, Orville had to fly a round-trip of ten miles from Fort Myer, Virginia, to Alexandria, Virginia, and back. About seven thousand people turned out to watch him take off with his passenger, Lieutenant Benjamin Foulois. The ride was a choppy one. At times Orville barely cleared the treetops.

Meanwhile, Wilbur waited anxiously at Fort Myer. It seemed to him that the flight was taking too long. Suddenly a cry rose from the crowd. "There it comes!" The Flyer landed to a burst of cheering and honking of horns. Grinning broadly, Wilbur raced to the scene. The brothers had done it! They had completed the army's requirements and sold their first plane to the U.S. government.

In August, Orville and Katharine went to Germany for more demonstration flights. Crowds of over 200,000 turned out to watch Orville fly. Crown Prince Friedrich Wilhelm was so thrilled at being taken aloft that he gave Orville his own stickpin set with a diamond W.

Wilbur wasn't having nearly as much fun in the United States. He was filing lawsuits against manufacturers who had illegally used the Wrights' patents. But he got his chance to take to the air again when he was asked to fly at a special celebration in New York. He circled the

Wilbur makes a pass over Governor's Island in New York Harbor during his circuit around the Statue of Liberty in September 1909.

Statue of Liberty and made a twenty-mile round-trip along the Hudson River while one million people watched from the shore.

The Wright brothers knew that flying machines would soon be more than a novelty. As Flyers improved in safety and design, aircraft would revolutionize transportation throughout the world. Wilbur and Orville prepared to meet the challenges of a new era by forming the Wright Company in November 1909. They opened an airplane factory and a flight school to train pilots. Among the staff, Orville was known for his humor, Wilbur for his keen observations. The men called Wilbur Eagle Eye because he spotted problems so instantly. One mechanic even said that Wilbur "could see through a brick wall." But Wilbur spent more of his time in court defending patents than he did on the field. Orville took on the task of daily supervision and encouraging the students.

Over the last few years, Wilbur and Orville had given many people the chance to fly, including Katharine, who had flown with Orville in Europe. There was still one very important individual waiting for a ride. On May 25, 1910, Orville finally took his eighty-one-year-old father up in a Flyer. Above the roar of the engine, the bishop yelled excitedly, "Higher, Orville. Higher!" Father and son soared up to 350 feet.

Wilbur and Orville still lived with Milton and Katharine on Hawthorn Street. Now that they were famous and rich, it seemed time to build a bigger house. They had already bought some land in a distinguished neighborhood when Wilbur returned home sick from a business trip.

A grieving Orville *(front with hat)* at Wilbur's funeral, in 1912. In his will, Wilbur left the bulk of his estate to Orville, "who has been associated with me in all the hopes and labors both of childhood and manhood."

Rallying a bit, he went with Orville and Katharine to visit the site of their future home. Afterward, however, his symptoms returned. He had typhoid fever.

Thirteen years earlier, Orville had survived a bout of the dangerous illness, but forty-five-year-old Wilbur was worn out from constant work and courtroom battles. He died, surrounded by his family, on May 30, 1912. Expressions of sympathy came from all over the world. "A short life, full of consequences," a heartbroken Milton wrote in his diary.

More than anyone else, Orville and Katharine mourned Wilbur's loss. They were very quiet in the days following his death. But both were determined to be brave, and Orville resolved to carry on the work he had begun with his brother. Shouldering his solitary burdens, Orville assumed the presidency of the Wright Company. He built the new house that the Wrights had been planning. And he completed work on a device that automatically balanced a plane for the pilot. On New Year's Eve 1913, Orville gave a public demonstration of the invention at Huffman Field. Holding his hands high in the air, he circled the area seven times.

Despite Orville's success, the Wright Company was losing out to other companies. Inventors were building on

The Wright family, sorely missing Wilbur, gather on the steps of the newly completed Hawthorn Hill home.

the Wrights' accomplishments and producing better air-
planes. Without Wilbur, Orville lacked the heart to com-
pete with his rivals. He was more interested in science
than business. In 1915 Orville sold the company. The
next year, he built his own small laboratory. One year after
that, he agreed to become a consulting engineer to another
airplane company. He even allowed the new enterprise to
use his name, becoming the Dayton-Wright Company.

The outbreak of World War I in 1914 had spurred the
rapid production of planes for military use. Orville
found himself working on an unmanned bombing craft in
1917, but he was deeply saddened by this turn of events.
The Wright brothers had imagined flying machines as

The Dayton-Wright Company received a contract to produce
four thousand warplanes and four hundred training planes
during World War I.

instruments of peace—not war. "No, I don't have any regrets about my part in the invention of the airplane," he said, "though no one could deplore more than I the destruction it has caused."

After the war, President Woodrow Wilson named Orville to the National Advisory Committee for Aeronautics. Orville also kept busy in his lab. With his friend James Jacobs, Orville invented a split flap to increase the lifting power of wings. The device would also slow the plane if it started to plunge down. In 1924 the pair received a patent on their work. It took twenty years, however, for airline officials to realize the importance of the mechanism.

A beloved American hero, Orville enjoyed his family, his homes in Dayton and Canada, and his St. Bernard dog named Scipio. The last patent he ever received was for a toy to amuse his grandnieces and grandnephews at Christmas. Called Flips and Flops, it featured two wooden clowns swinging on a trapeze. Orville also liked to invent clever, laborsaving gadgets to help his home run smoothly. He enjoyed music and spent a great deal of time trying to develop a mechanism that would automatically change records on his phonograph. In the process, he broke so many records that he had to go begging for more from his relatives.

By this time, of course, the car had long replaced the bicycle as his daily mode of transportation. Orville drove so fast that the police "closed their eyes and held their breath" when he went by. And he still loved a good prank as much as ever. A faint smile and a twitch of his mustache usually signaled the beginning of a joke.

"We enjoyed his teasing as much as he did," a friend wrote, "for we learned that he only teased those he cared for."

Despite his fame and his many friends, Orville was still shy. He rarely gave speeches, and he hated to trouble anyone. When Franklin Roosevelt visited Dayton in 1940, Orville was invited to join the president in a ride around the city. Afterward the presidential limousine began to turn up the winding hill to Orville's home. Immediately Orville stopped the driver and got out of the car. There was no need, he felt, for the president to lose time by delivering him to the doorstep. After this incident, his family turned the tables on Orville and teased him.

(From left to right) President Franklin Delano Roosevelt, Orville Wright, and others in the presidential limousine in 1940

In his seventies, Orville remained active and full of ideas. After suffering a heart attack in October 1947, he was back in his lab by early November. But on January 27, 1948, he suffered a second attack. As his condition worsened, he remained thoughtful and attentive to his family and friends, and he kept his sense of humor, joking with the nurses. He died on January 30, 1948, at the age of seventy-seven. The entire world mourned the loss of the famous aviation pioneer eulogized by a local clergyman as "just one of folks like us."

Aviation had changed dramatically since the Wright brothers' first hazardous glides. In his last interview, Orville was asked if he ever imagined his work would lead to the modern airline industry. Laughing, he replied, "Not at all. We—my brother Wilbur and I—did it for fun. We got interested in the problem of whether it was possible to fly and we kept at it because we wanted to see if we could work it out." In working through their self-imposed challenge, the brothers ushered in the age of aviation and changed the world forever.

A Quarrel

with the Smithsonian

In 1914 two aviators, Albert Zahm and Glenn Curtiss, set out to prove that Wilbur and Orville Wright did not deserve full credit as inventors of the first airplane. They believed that Samuel Langley's Aerodrome, which had crashed days before the Wrights' first successful power flight in 1903, was actually a workable flying machine. Instead of restoring the Aerodrome to its original 1903 design, however, they altered the wings and other important features. With these changes, the craft was able to make a few short hops of about 150 feet. Curtiss continued to alter the machine, replacing the original engine with a modern one of his own design. This change finally enabled the Aerodrome to fly.

Zahm and Curtiss kept their changes from the world. The Smithsonian, which had sponsored their work, accepted the test results and displayed the Aerodrome with the caption: "The first man-carrying aeroplane in the history of the world capable of sustained free flight."

Orville was furious that the Smithsonian would deny him and his brother rightful credit for their accomplishment.

The Curtiss-Zahm Aerodrome of 1914
(above) was not an exact replica of Samuel
Langley's aircraft of 1903, as Glenn
Curtiss (inset) and Albert Zahm claimed.

Finally in 1925, frustrated by the Smithsonian's position, Orville sent the 1903 Flyer to be displayed in the Science Museum of London. Many Americans were shocked and disappointed. Orville explained, "In a foreign museum this machine will be a constant reminder of the reasons for its being there, and after the people and petty jealousies of this day are gone, the historians of the future may examine the evidence impartially and make history accord with it."

The Smithsonian wanted the 1903 Wright Flyer for its collection, but it refused to concede its position until 1943. At that time, the institution published the differences between the Aerodrome of 1903 and the version of 1914.

The "whopper flying machine" on display. About 850
people crammed into a hall at the Smithsonian to view
the dedication of the 1903 Flyer on December 17, 1948.
President Harry S. Truman took part in the ceremony.

Satisfied with this admission, Orville wrote to the
Museum of London asking that the plane be returned to
the United States. However, World War II (1939–1945)
delayed the return for several years.

The Flyer was unveiled December 17, 1948, the forty-
fifth anniversary of its successful flights at Kitty Hawk.
A ceremony that honored the Wright brothers and gave

them full credit for the first heavier-than-air, sustained, powered flight was attended by 850 people. Suspended from the ceiling, surrounded by historical aircraft of all kinds, the Flyer has become one of the most popular exhibits at the Smithsonian Air and Space Museum.

To the Moon

In 1969 another American hero remembered the Wright brothers' persistence and courage. Astronaut Neil Armstrong carried a small wood fragment and tiny piece of cloth from the 1903 Flyer aboard *Apollo 11*. It was a reminder of how far flight science had advanced and a tribute to two men who never imagined a keepsake from their handiwork would travel to the moon.

THE MECHANICS OF FLIGHT

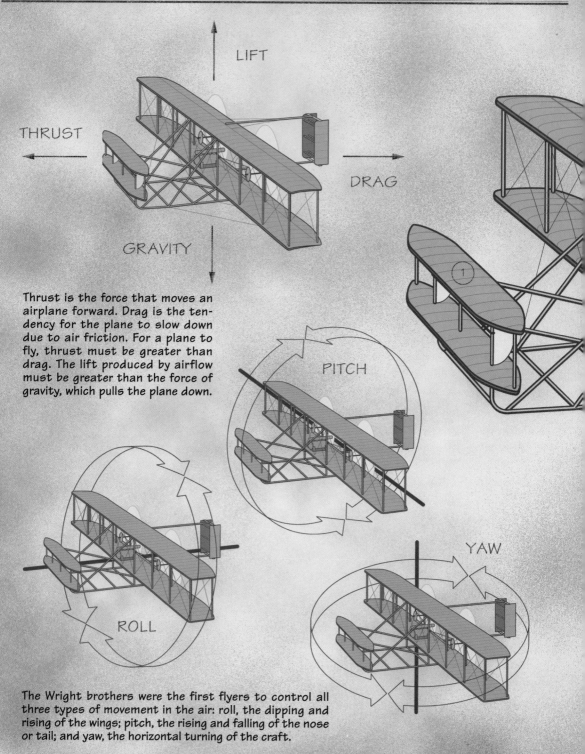

LIFT

THRUST

DRAG

GRAVITY

Thrust is the force that moves an airplane forward. Drag is the tendency for the plane to slow down due to air friction. For a plane to fly, thrust must be greater than drag. The lift produced by airflow must be greater than the force of gravity, which pulls the plane down.

PITCH

ROLL

YAW

The Wright brothers were the first flyers to control all three types of movement in the air: roll, the dipping and rising of the wings; pitch, the rising and falling of the nose or tail; and yaw, the horizontal turning of the craft.

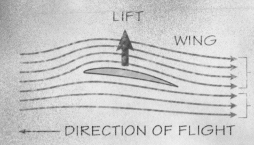

LIFT
WING

Airflow **over** wing: LONGER PATH, FASTER, LOWER PRESSURE

Airflow **under** wing: SHORTER PATH, SLOWER, HIGHER PRESSURE. This greater upward pressure causes the wing to rise into the air.

← DIRECTION OF FLIGHT

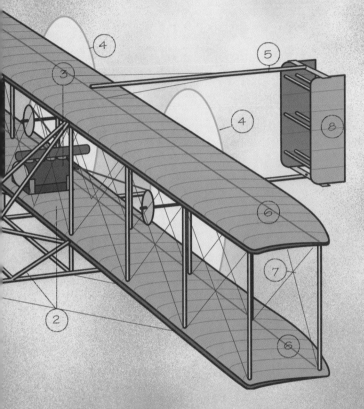

The Wright 1905 Flyer

1. Elevator (front)
2. Frame skids and horizontal passenger space
3. Engine
4. Propellers
5. Rudder control arms
6. Upper and lower warpable wings
7. Wing struts
8. Moveable rudder (rear)

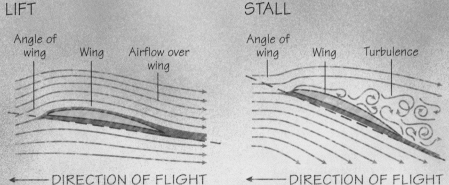

LIFT

Angle of wing   Wing   Airflow over wing

← DIRECTION OF FLIGHT

STALL

Angle of wing   Wing   Turbulence

← DIRECTION OF FLIGHT

When a wing angles upward too steeply, turbulence develops. Airflow across the wing is broken, and lift decreases. This causes the airplane to stall.

Source Notes

p. 8 Marvin W. McFarland, ed., *The Papers of Wilbur and Orville Wright,* vol. 1, *1899–1905,* (New York: McGraw-Hill, 1953), 400.

> Bishop Milton Wright to Carl Dienstbach, Dayton, December 22, 1903.

p. 8 Fred C. Kelly, *The Wright Brothers: A Biography* (1943; reprint, New York: Dover Publications, 1989), 28.

> First published in 1943 as *The Wright Brothers: A Biography Authorized by Orville Wright.*

p. 9 Tom D. Crouch, *The Bishop's Boys: A Life of Wilbur and Orville Wright* (New York: W. W. Norton & Company, 1989), 48.

p. 13 Kelly, *The Wright Brothers,* 8.

p. 21 Crouch, *The Bishop's Boys,* 96.

> Taken from a recollection by Ed Sines in *Popular Aviation,* June 1938.

p. 21 Charlotte K. and August E. Brunsman, *The Other Career of Wilbur and Orville: Wright & Wright, Printers* (Kettering, OH: Trailside Press, 1989), 9.

p. 22 Crouch, *The Bishop's Boys,* 77.

p. 22 Brunsman, *The Other Career of Wilbur and Orville,* 9.

p. 22 Crouch, *The Bishop's Boys,* 97.

p. 23 Ibid., 106.

> According to Crouch: "The two young men who had constructed printing presses from scratch were already legendary mechanics on the West Side. Now they found themselves besieged by friends in need of bicycle repairs. The second business for which they had been searching was literally thrust upon them."

p. 25 Ibid., 113.

> Taken from *Snap-Shots,* April 17, 1896.

p. 27 Peter L. Jakob, *Visions of a Flying Machine: The Wright Brothers and the Process of Invention* (Washington, D.C.: Smithsonian Institution Press, 1990), 40.

p. 28 Kelly, *The Wright Brothers,* 44.

> On p. 45, Kelly states the brothers' view that Lilienthal's gliding "must be the king of sports, to go soaring through the air on a gliding machine."

p. 33 McFarland, *The Papers of Wilbur and Orville Wright,* 3.

p. 33 Crouch, *The Bishop's Boys,* 161.

> On p. 165, Crouch states that Wilbur's understanding actually surpassed that of his peers. "Wilbur spent three months, from June to August 1899, sifting through the chaff of aeronautical history and theory to arrive at a far more accurate understanding of the state of the art than men like Langley and Chanute who had spent decades in the field and written books on the subject."

p. 35 Ibid., 172.

> Crouch quotes Wilbur's testimony from a patent infringement suit: "Here was the silent birth that underlies all human flight."

p. 38 Fred C. Kelly, ed., *Miracle at Kitty Hawk: The Letters of Wilbur & Orville Wright* (1951; reprint, New York: Da Capo Press, 1996), 22.

p. 40 Ibid., 26.

p. 42 Ibid., 27.

p. 43 McFarland, *The Papers of Wilbur and Orville Wright*, 24.

p. 44 Kelly, *Miracle at Kitty Hawk*, 30.

p. 45 John Evangelist Walsh, *One Day at Kitty Hawk: The Untold Story of the Wright Brothers and the Airplane* (New York: Thomas Y. Crowell Company, 1975), 52.

p. 46 McFarland, *The Papers of Wilbur and Orville Wright*, 38.

p. 46 Kelly, *Miracle at Kitty Hawk*, 35.

p. 47 Fred C. Howard, *Wilbur and Orville: A Biography of the Wright Brothers* (Mineola, NY: Dover Publications, 1998), 53.

p. 48 Peter L. Jakob and Rick Young, eds., *The Published Writings of Wilbur and Orville Wright* (Washington, D.C.: Smithsonian Institution Press, 2000), 286.

> From Charles E. Taylor, as told to Robert S. Ball, "My Story of the Wright Brothers."

p. 49 Crouch, *The Bishop's Boys*, 207.

p. 49 McFarland, *The Papers of Wilbur and Orville Wright*, 73.

p. 49 Crouch, *The Bishop's Boys*, 208.

p. 50 Howard, *Wilbur and Orville*, 63.

p. 53 McFarland, *The Papers of Wilbur and Orville Wright*, 116.

p. 54 Howard, *Wilbur and Orville*, 69.

p. 54 Crouch, *The Bishop's Boys*, 219.

p. 56 Ivonette Wright Miller, comp., *Wright Reminiscences* (Wright-Patterson Air Force Base, OH: The Air Force Museum Foundation, 1978), 60.

p. 56 Kelly, *Miracle at Kitty Hawk*, 20.

p. 57 Miller, *Wright Reminiscences*, 61.

p. 57 Ibid., 2.

> Milton Wright writes: "The matter-of-fact way in which my uncles used the gadgets and planed the spruce strips and glued them together into ribs for their "flying machine" left me with the impression that all bicycle shops did the same thing. It was all very commonplace."

p. 59 McFarland, *The Papers of Wilbur and Orville Wright*, 260.

> From Orville Wright's diary.

p. 59 Ibid.

p. 60 Kelly, *Miracle at Kitty Hawk*, 80.

p. 60 Howard, *Wilbur and Orville*, 87–88.

p. 63 McFarland, *The Papers of Wilbur and Orville Wright,* 280.

> More completely, Orville wrote: "Day before yesterday we had a wind of 16 miles per second or about 30 miles per hour, and glided in it without any trouble. That was the highest wind a gliding machine was ever in so that we now hold all the records! The largest machine we handled in any kind [of weather], made the longest distance glide (American), the longest time in the air, the smallest angle of descent, and the highest wind!!!"

p. 64 Crouch, *The Bishop's Boys,* 243.

p. 64 McFarland, *The Papers of Wilbur and Orville Wright,* 313.

p. 66 Kelly, *Miracle at Kitty Hawk,* 105–106.

> From a letter from Orville to Katharine, November 1, 1903.

p. 67 Ibid., 106.

p. 67 McFarland, *The Papers of Wilbur and Orville Wright,* 367.

p. 67 Howard, *Wilbur and Orville,* 115.

p. 67 McFarland, *The Papers of Wilbur and Orville Wright,* 380.

p. 68 Howard, *Wilbur and Orville,* 121.

p. 70 Crouch, *The Bishop's Boys,* 265.

p. 71 Jakob and Young, *The Published Writings,* 276.

p. 73 Ibid.

p. 73 Orville Wright, *How We Invented the Airplane: An Illustrated History,* ed. Fred C. Kelly (New York: Dover Publications, 1953), 21.

p. 74 McFarland, *The Papers of Wilbur and Orville Wright,* 411.

p. 74 Jakob and Young, *The Published Writings,* 56.

> Wilbur's statement made to the magazine *Boys' Life* in 1914 reads: "My brother and I were not excited nor particularly exultant. We had been the first to fly successfully with a machine driven by an engine, but we had expected to be the first. We had known deep down in our hearts, that the machine would fly just as it did. The proof was not astonishing to us. We were simply glad, that's all."

p. 74 Crouch, *The Bishop's Boys,* 270.

p. 79 Kelly, *The Wright Brothers,* 128.

> According to Kelly, the new launch system allowed the brothers to take off "even in a dead calm."

p. 79 Richard P. Hallion, ed., *The Wright Brothers: Heirs of Prometheus* (Washington, D.C.: National Air and Space Museum, 1978), 115.

> Includes the full eyewitness account by Amos Root.

p. 82 Kelly, *The Wright Brothers,* 178.

p. 84 Crouch, *The Bishop's Boys,* 315.

> On p. 303, Crouch states that the brothers "would not allow anyone, even a potential buyer, to witness a flight or even see the machine, until a contract was signed. Nor would they provide interested parties with photographs, drawings, or technical descriptions of any kind."

p. 86 Ibid., 356.

p. 88 Kelly, *The Wright Brothers,* 238.
      Author translated the phrases from French.

p. 89 Miller, *Wright Reminiscences,* 6.

p. 89 Kelly, *The Wright Brothers,* 245.

p. 89 Ibid., 27.

p. 90 Mark Bernstein, *Grand Eccentrics: Turning the Century: Dayton and the Inventing of America* (Wilmington, OH: Orange Frazer Press, 1996), 114.

p. 91 Kelly, *Miracle at Kitty Hawk,* 311.
      Letter is dated Le Mans, September 13, 1908.

p. 93 Ibid., 315.
      Wilbur writes to Katharine on September 20, 1908: "The death of poor Selfridge was a greater shock to me than Orville's injuries, severe as the latter were. I felt sure 'Bubbo' would pull through all right, but the other was irremediable."

p. 93 Crouch, *The Bishop's Boys,* 378.

p. 94 Miller, *Wright Reminiscences,* 159.

p. 95 Kelly, *The Wright Brothers,* 253.
      Kelly quotes an English duke, Lord Northcliffe, on the Wrights: "I never knew more simple, unaffected people than Wilbur, Orville, and Katharine. . . . I don't think the excitement and interest produced by their extraordinary feat had any effect on them."

p. 97 Howard, *Wilbur and Orville,* 306.

p. 99 Bernstein, *Grand Eccentrics,* 125.

p. 99 Crouch, *The Bishop's Boys,* 12.

p. 100 Fred C. Fisk, and Marlin W. Todd, *The Wright Brothers: From Bicycle to Biplane,* (West Milton, OH: Miami Graphic Services, 2000), 87.

p. 100 Crouch., *The Bishop's Boys,* 12.

p. 103 Jakob and Young, *The Published Writings,* 261.
      From an interview with Orville Wright by Fred Kelly that appeared in the *St. Louis Post-Dispatch*, November 7, 1943.

p. 103 Miller, *Wright Reminiscences,* 16.

p. 104 Ibid., 141.

p. 105 Crouch, *The Bishop's Boys,* 525.

p. 105 Jakob and Young, *The Published Writings,* 98.
      From an interview with Orville Wright by Leland D. Case, in *The Rotarian,* April 1948.

p. 106 Crouch, *The Bishop's Boys,* 487.

p. 107 Jakob and Young, *The Published Writings,* 96.
      Taken from *U.S. Air Services,* February 1948.

Selected Bibliography

Books

Bernstein, Mark. *Grand Eccentrics: Turning the Century: Dayton and the Inventing of America.* Wilmington, OH: Orange Frazer Press, 1996.

Combs, Harry, and Martin Caidin. *Kill Devil Hill: Discovering the Secret of the Wright Brothers.* Boston: Houghton Mifflin, 1979.

Crouch, Tom D. *The Bishop's Boys: A Life of Wilbur and Orville Wright.* New York: W. W. Norton & Company, 1989.

Culick, Fred E. C., and Spencer Dunmore. *On Great White Wings: The Wright Brothers and the Race for Flight.* New York: Hyperion, 2001.

DuFour, H. R., and Peter J. Unitt. *Charles E. Taylor, 1868–1956: The Wright Brothers Mechanician.* Dayton, OH: 1997.

Fisk, Fred C., and Marlin W. Todd. *The Wright Brothers: From Bicycle to Biplane.* West Milton, OH: Miami Graphic Services 2000.

Freedman, Russell. *The Wright Brothers: How They Invented the Airplane.* New York: Holiday House, 1991.

Geibert, Ronald R., and Patrick B. Nolan. *Kitty Hawk and Beyond: The Wright Brothers and the Early Years of Aviation.* Dayton, OH: Wright State University Press, 1990.

Hallion, Richard P., ed. *The Wright Brothers: Heirs of Prometheus.* Washington, D.C.: Smithsonian Institution Press, 1978.

Howard, Fred C. *Wilbur and Orville: A Biography of the Wright Brothers.* Mineola, NY: Dover Publications, 1998.

Jakob, Peter L. *Visions of a Flying Machine: The Wright Brothers and the Process of Invention.* Washington, D.C.: Smithsonian Institution Press, 1990.

Jakob, Peter L., and Rick Young, eds. *The Published Writings of Wilbur and Orville Wright.* Washington, D.C.: Smithsonian Institution Press, 2000.

Kelly, Fred C. *Miracle at Kitty Hawk: The Letters of Wilbur & Orville Wright.* 1951. Reprint, New York: Da Capo Press, 1996.

———. *The Wright Brothers: A Biography.* 1943. Reprint, New York: Dover Publications, 1989.

McFarland, Marvin W., ed. *The Papers of Wilbur and Orville Wright.* 2 vols. New York: McGraw-Hill, 1953.

Miller, Ivonette Wright, comp. *Wright Reminiscences.* Wright-Patterson AFB, OH: The Air Force Museum Foundation, 1978.

Walsh, John Evangelist. *One Day at Kitty Hawk: The Untold Story of the Wright Brothers and the Aeroplane.* New York: Crowell, 1975.

Wright, Orville. *How We Invented the Airplane: An Illustrated History.* ed. Fred C. Riley. New York: Dover Publications, 1953.

Booklets and Magazines

Brunsman, Charlotte K., and August E. Brunsman. *The Other Career of Wilbur and Orville: Wright & Wright, Printers.* Kettering, OH: Trailside Press, 1989.

Crouch, Tom D. *The Wright Brothers at Carillon Historical Park.* Dayton, OH: Carillon Historical Park, 1993.

McMahon, John R. "The Real Fathers of Flight." *Popular Science Monthly,* January–June, 1929.

1905 Wright Flyer III, *The First Practical Airplane.* Dayton, OH: Carillon Historical Park and Wright State University, n.d.

OTHER RESOURCES

Websites

The American Experience/The Wright Stuff. 2003.
  <http://www. pbs.org/wgbh/amex/wright>

Honoring the Wright Brothers: The AIAA Wright Flyer Project. 2003.
  <http://www.wrightflyer.org>, <http://www.wright-brothers.org>

Re-Living the Wright Way—NASA. 2003.
  <http://wright.nasa.gov>

Welcome—The First Flight Society. 2003.
  <http://www.firstflight. org>

Wright Brothers Aeroplane Company and Museum of Pioneer Aviation. 2003.
  <http://www.first-to-fly.com>

INDEX

Maxin, Sir Hiram, 31
moon voyage, 109

National Advisory Committee for Aeronautics, 103
Newton's Third Law of Motion, 64

Osborn, Agnes, 26

patents, 82–83, 84, 85, 98, 99, 103
Pénaud helicopter (toy), 13–14, 28
Perry, Israel, 42–43
pitch, definition of, 62–63
printing and printing press, 16, 17, 20–21
propellers, 67, 68, 69, 93: mechanics of, 64

roll, definition of, 62
Roosevelt, President Franklin, 104
Roosevelt Jr., Teddy, 89
Root, Amos, 79
Ruse, Cordy, 28

Selfridge, Lieutenant Thomas, 92–93
7 Hawthorn Street, 10, 17, 25–26, 53, 99
Sines, Ed, 17
Smithsonian Institution, the, 32, 33, 106–109
Snap-Shots, 25
Spratt, George, 50, 59, 64
Stauffer, Amos, 82

Taft, President William, 96
Tate, Dan, 50
Tate, William (Bill), 40, 44, 45, 47, 50
Tate family, 43
Taylor, Charlie, 48, 63, 64, 67, 68

United States Army. *See* United States government contract
United States government contract, 83, 102: requirements for, 85, 86, 89, 93, 96–97

well digging, 60–62
Western Society of Engineers, 54
West Side News, 21–22
Wilhelm, Crown Prince Friedrich, 98
Wilson, President Woodrow, 103
wings, mechanics of, 34, 35–36, 38, 53, 54–56, 58, 103
World War I, 102
Wright, Horace, 57
Wright, Ida, 10
Wright, Ivonette, 57
Wright, Katharine, 10, 11, 15, 19, 25–27, 43, 46, 49, 54, 67, 93, 94–95, 98, 99–101
Wright, Leontine, 57
Wright, Lorin, 9, 10, 18, 27, 57, 59, 75, 76
Wright, Milton, 8–9, 11, 12–13, 14, 16–17, 21–22, 25–27, 42, 57–58, 99, 100
Wright, Orville: birth, 10; childhood, 10–17; death, 105; *Evening Item,* 22; flight demonstrations in Germany, 8, 98; Fort Myer, Virginia, flight demonstrations, 89–93; in France, 94–95; illness, 29, 31; injury, 92–93; kites and kite making, 15; later years, 103–105; printing and printing press, 16, 17, 20–21; and the Smithsonian Institution, 106–109; *West Side News,* 21–22
Wright, Otis, 10
Wright, Reuchlin, 9, 10, 18, 27